DATE DUE

Class

Concepts in Social Thought

Series Editor: Frank Parkin

Published Titles

Concepts in Social Thought

Class

Richard Scase

University of Minnesota Press

Minneapolis

Published by the University of Minnesota Press
2037 University Avenue Southeast, Minneapolis, MN 55414

Printed in Great Britain by J. W. Arrowsmith Ltd, Bristol

Library of Congress Cataloging-in-Publication Data

Scase, Richard.
    Class/Richard Scase.
        p.   cm. – (Concepts in social thought)
    Includes bibliographical references.
    ISBN 0–8166–2148–9 (hc). – ISBN 0–8166–2149–7 (pb)
    1. Social classes.   I. Title.   II. Series.
HT609.S33   1992
305.5 – dc20   91–39797
                                                                    CIP

Contents

Preface

The invitation to contribute to a series such as this compels any author to choose between a number of possible approaches. One is to offer the reader a comprehensive review of the relevant literature. Another is to use the opportunity to make a fundamental statement, offering an innovative approach towards a key issue. I have chosen neither of these. Instead, I have accepted the Editor's invitation to offer an introduction, albeit brief, to the analysis of social class. Essentially, I aim to demonstrate the continuing importance of class analysis in sociological discussion, despite popular assumptions that it is of declining relevance and irrespective of recent developments in Eastern Europe and the Soviet Union. This book, then, tries to restate the continuing importance of class for those students who have only recently discovered the intellectual challenges and excitement of sociological analysis.

1
The Relevance of Class

Of all the concepts used by sociologists for describing and explaining social relationships, social class is probably the most ambiguous, confusing and ill-defined. This is despite the fact that the development of sociology as an academic discipline in Europe has been intimately connected with the analysis of class-related issues. Indeed, the study of social class is so central that almost any discussion that does not, in one way or another, offer explanations with reference to it is often viewed by sociologists as deficient. Even so, analyses of class continue to be shrouded in as much ambiguity and uncertainty as they were decades ago because of imprecision of definition and terminology.

It may be suggested that the central role of social class within sociological explanations has reinforced the excessively academic nature of the discipline, with few non-specialists able to grasp more than a little understanding of what *is* exactly *meant* by notions of social class. Whereas sociologists will often, first and foremost, describe identities, interpersonal relationships and social institutions by reference to social class, this is usually not the case for the non-specialist lay person. The latter is more likely to refer to personal descriptions in terms of such factors as age, gender, occupation, ethnicity, family and place of residence. Very rarely will reference be made to social class and even if it is, it will tend to be in a relatively superficial manner. As respondents in social surveys will often state, 'class is not as important as it used to be', 'most people are "middle class" nowadays', and 'everyone now is working class. Even the aristocracy have to work for their living' [*sic*].

Sociology, as a discipline devoted to the description and under-standing of social relationships, is faced with a major dilemma. The very concept that is central to its method of analysis is perceived as largely irrelevant by actors in the 'real world'. Yet sociology professes to be an empirical discipline committed to formulating testable hypotheses which, on the basis of systematic research, can enhance the understanding of social relationships. It attempts to achieve this through the use of class concepts that are perceived by non-sociologists as relatively irrelevant. It is hardly surprising that the standing of the subject as an explanatory discipline is often considered to be questionable.

Should sociologists reconsider their theoretical and analytical positions in order to offer explanations without such a heavy recourse to notions of class? Currently, there seem to be two major orientations towards the use of class categories among sociologists. There are those who, following Marx's ideas, regard the inherent antagonisms of class relationships to be the vehicles of social change. For them, it is necessary to identify the determinants of class membership (Carchedi, 1975; Poulantzas, 1975; Wright 1985). Normally only *two* classes are permitted, although allowance is sometimes given for other residual or peripheral class categories. According to the criteria of class adopted, occupations are sifted and sorted into class categories. There is then a search for class consciousness – as measured in terms of socio-political beliefs or class self-placement – in order to demonstrate the continuing salience of class subjectivity in modern society. Such writers proceed to argue that it is only the absence of an appropriate political agency – normally a role given to the Labour Party in Britain or social democratic parties in Europe – that prevents the working class from becoming a major force for revolutionary social change (Korpi, 1983). That such change has not already occurred is usually interpreted to be the result of ideological and organizational failings of these political agencies and their inability to nurture the latent class consciousness of their *natural* class supporters.

If many accounts are not as *explicit* in their orientations as this, their implicit assumptions and underlying frames of reference none the less adhere to such a perspective. Unfortunately, they mean little to the lay person because most people do not relate to, identify with or see themselves as members of social classes, except possibly in superficial ways. Of course, elements of class consciousness can be found among respondents in social surveys. If interviewers probe and explicitly make reference to class categories, it is likely that comments will be made by correspondents that can be interpreted as evidence of class consciousness. But this, surely, is far removed from what Marx had in mind. However, such data have often been seized upon as evidence that the working class remains an agent of revolutionary or, at least, reformist social change.

There are others who approach issues of class from a much more empirical perspective, attempting to describe the world *as it is* rather than as they would like it to be (Marshall *et al.*, 1988). Again there is a tendency to construct concepts of class by combining (and sometimes splitting) various occupational categories. In such analyses, there are normally three steps in the research investigation. First, information is obtained about respondents' jobs in terms of their titles, duties, earnings and so on. These jobs are then allocated to various occupational categories, such as 'higher managerial and professional', 'routine non-manual' or 'semi-skilled manual'. Finally, such occupational groupings are distributed to a number of so-called social classes. Thus, respondents who have completed census questionnaires or provided interviewers with details about their jobs, often in the most vague terms, find that they have become members of a particular social class. Such a procedure has become even more complicated in recent decades because of the increasing numbers of married women who are now employed. This has generated debate as to whether or not these women should occupy *independent* class positions or those determined by the occupations of their partners (Goldthorpe, 1983; Erikson, 1984; Stanworth, 1984). But is this a relevant empirical issue if class membership *itself* is a function of predetermined categories constructed by investigators, to which jobs and occupations are allocated? Because of this research process it is, of course, hardly surprising that the consequent class groupings are characterized by a great deal of heterogeneity in terms of socio-political attitudes and life-styles. Indeed, such 'empirical' definitions of social class are often little more than statistical artifacts that produce even more vague and ambiguous descriptions of social reality than their constituent occupational categories. What is the point of collapsing occupational categories that are, in fact, more meaningful in everyday life into more ambiguous and imprecise class groupings? If sociologists are interested in describing patterns of behaviour in ways perceived as relevant and meaningful, occupational categories are probably more appropriate than aggregated social classes (Marshall *et al.*, 1988).

Are we to argue that concepts of social class, although central to sociological explanations, are largely redundant? Further, does such an over-emphasis 'marginalize' sociology, both as an analytical academic discipline and as a provider of data for various practitioners? Certainly, the use of class terminology and class categories for the purposes of data analysis inhibits rather than facilitates dialogue between sociologists and others. Even in terms of discussion within the discipline, the Marxist-inspired debates of the late 1970s about issues of 'class boundaries' and 'contradictory class locations' now seem somewhat sterile (Parkin, 1979). Such debates may have generated heated discourse within seminar rooms and lecture theatres but the political reality was the election of rightist regimes in a number of Western countries. What, then, is the relevance of *class* within contemporary sociological analysis and is it of any help in our understanding of social structure and processes?

Despite the ambiguity of definition and the generally perceived lack of relevance of class as a source of personal identity in everyday life, it can be argued that it continues to be crucial for any detailed understanding of the dynamics of Western capitalist society. Although the everyday expression of class-related processes is rarely evident, the underlying structural forces of capitalist countries reaffirm the value of social class as one of the major explanatory social processes – but only if and when social class is conceived and understood within a specific Marxist analytical and empirical perspective. It is only within such a frame of reference that notions of social class have any bearing upon the understanding of modern society. This is because Western societies are fundamentally *capitalist* and, as a result, no understanding of their institutions, structures and processes can be complete without an analysis of classes as constituents of objective social relationships. It is, then, necessary to specify the more detailed criteria according to which the concept of social class is to be understood. In order to do this, it is pertinent to discuss Marx's ideas on capitalism as a mode of production.

According to Marx, it is possible to identify various modes of production as they have existed in history (Marx and Engels, 1964). He refers to these as the *Asiatic*, the *feudal* and the *capitalist* with each characterized by specific forces and social relations of production. In the Asiatic, as it existed in ancient India, for instance, there is little or no economic surplus and production barely meets the rudimentary needs of producers. There is little differentiation between producers and non-producers and, accordingly, very little in the form of a social division of labour or economic inequalities. Since there is virtually no economic surplus, private property ownership is almost non-existent because there is no expropriation of the economic surplus by non-producers. Societies such as these, which are little more than self-sustaining in their levels of economic production, are characterized by the absence of class relations. There is no material basis for the formation of antagonistic social groupings since all forms of economic production are consumed in common. It is only with developments in the technical forces of production and, with this, the emergence of a division of labour that it is feasible for an economic surplus to be generated. Only then are there the pre-conditions for exploitative social relations within which the non-producers – that is, the owners of the technical forces of production – are able to expropriate the generated economic surplus. In these circumstances, as found in agrarian societies, such relations of expropriation constitute the basis for the formation of *objective* social classes. Privately owned property is the inevitable outcome of class-based exploitation, as witnessed, according to Marx, in the material and cultural differences of the nobility and the peasantry under feudalism and the bourgeoisie and the proletariat within capitalism (Marx and Engels, 1969).

From a Marxist perspective, any understanding of class must be located within an analysis of economic production and the processes whereby this is distributed, consumed and expropriated. It has little to do with the allocation of occupations into class categories or with the ranking of such occupations into status or income hierarchies. If the study of occupations does have any relevance for class analysis, it is because they are the expression of social relations as found within the productive process. Class theory, then, is solely relevant for the study of productive relations that are essentially exploitative and antagonistic between, on the one hand, the producers of economic surplus and, on the other, the non-producers who privately own the means of production (Marx and Engels, 1969). As such, class relationships refer, in any mode of production, to patterns of ownership and control. Within each mode of production there are producers who create the economic surplus, which is then expropriated to become the private property and wealth of the non-producers. It is this relationship that, according to Marx, constitutes the essential antagonism of the capitalist mode of production and that is the overriding structural basis for conflict and struggle between the two great classes: the proletariat and the bourgeoisie. For him, they are the predominant forces of social change because the irreconcilable nature of class antagonism can only lead to the destruction of the mode of production. Hence, for Marx, all history is the history of class struggles, with each mode of production containing the seeds of its own destruction. It is only with the transition from capitalism to socialism that production ceases to be organized upon an exploitative and antagonistic basis (Marx and Engels, 1969). Marx's theory of social change, therefore, hinges upon his theory of social class – a position that is rather different from approaches that utilize notions of class for the purposes of discussing aggregates or clusters of attitudes and behaviour in society. Should, then, class theories be retained and used *solely* for the purposes of describing productive relations as these are found within capitalist society? Perhaps the desirability of such an approach can be illuminated by discussing Marx's ideas in more detail. In this way, it will be possible to demonstrate the continuing relevance of *class* for the analysis of contemporary capitalist social structures.

According to Marx, within a given mode of production there can be only two predominant classes, consisting of those who produce and those who expropriate the economic surplus. Although the relationship between these two classes is antagonistic, they are mutually interdependent. The dominant class can only expropriate if there is a subordinate class that produces the economic surplus. However, because this relationship is unstable it is necessary for the non-producer class – the bourgeoisie under capitalism – to legiti-mate its exploitative position. This is undertaken through a variety of ideological and cultural processes which, in constituting the 'superstructure' of society, conceal the exploitative nature of class relations, grounded as these are within the material 'base' of the mode of production (Marx, 1975).

It is in this context that Marx differentiates between notions of *class in itself* and *class for itself*. Objective class relations only develop into forms of consciousness when producers become aware of their exploited position in society. It is this lack of consciousness that has led to claims that social class, as a sociological phenomenon, has become redundant. However, such arguments overlook the fact that, by definition, classes exist as a feature of *objective* reality if only because of the very existence of capitalist society. Capitalism cannot function without social classes; equally there can be no social classes without capitalism. Hence, it is always possible to refer to *class in itself* because of the antagonistic nature of the social relations of production. The *subjective* experiences of the participating actors constitute related but, nevertheless, quite different issues for enquiry. How is such a perspective to be applied to the analysis of contemporary capitalist society? It is necessary to outline, if only briefly, Marx's ideas on the development of capitalism.

In his discussions, Marx draws heavily upon developments as they occurred in Britain after the sixteenth century (Marx, 1974). He explains how the capitalization of ground rent, the enclosure system and the growth of trading created the pre-conditions for merchant and then later industrial capitalism. As wealth became concentrated among landlords and merchants, a process of *capital accumulation* evolved whereby commodities were produced for profitable sale in the market-place. Merchant capital was transferred into various rural-based industries, such as spinning and weaving, generating the pre-conditions for various forms of simple commodity production. But, for Marx, this was pre-capitalist in its character because producers were *independent* artisans, each of whom performed a variety of all-round skills. There was little or no division of labour and if there was a rudimentary breakdown of tasks this was between men and women, and adults and children within the family system. The family, then, constituted the unit of economic production, within which craft workers owned the technical means of production. Gradually, however, the merchants extended their control over these producers through the 'putting-out' system, whereby they delivered the raw materials, extended credit and then collected the finished products. Thus, the producers became increasingly dependent upon merchants for the supply of their raw materials, work and, hence, livelihood. It is at this stage in the development of production relations that Marx suggests there is the emergence of the capitalist mode of production proper. Merchants become full-blown capitalists, there is the gradual destruction of the putting-out system, and the factory becomes the predominant means of production. In his discussion of the factory system Marx identifies three stages in the development of the capitalist mode of production: *cooperation*, *manufacture* and *modern industry*.

The first stage, cooperation, is characterized by the concentration of producers in small workshops; in other words, production is removed from the family household and constitutes the real beginnings of capitalist social relations. As Marx states: 'labourers working together, at the same time, in one place . . . in order to produce the same sort of commodity under the mastership of one capitalist, constitutes, both historically and logically, the starting-point of capitalist production' (Marx, 1974, p. 305). Even so, Marx recognized that, other than the transference of production from the household to the workshop, there was often little change in the nature and performance of work tasks since artisans continued to exercise a variety of skills in their productive work.

This stage is rapidly superseded by that of manufacture, within which the distinctive classes of capitalists and producers become more visible. Under manufacture, there is the appearance of a detailed division of labour within which each producer, under the more direct commands of capitalist owners, undertakes only a limited range of tasks. The production of commodities then becomes a *social process*, with each worker dependent upon capitalists for his or her livelihood since the latter own not only the factories but also all the other technical means of production. Hence, the producers' contribution to the work process is solely in terms of their *labour power*. This is exchanged for wages which they then spend upon their subsistence needs. At the stage of manufacture, then, there emerge the 'two great classes' of capitalism: the owners of the means of production and producers who, as wage labourers, are alienated from both the means of production and the product of their labour. Capitalists pay wages so that workers are able to live at a socially determined level of subsistence and for this outlay they receive, in return, the production of goods that have a *market* or *exchange* value which is greater than the outlay they have expended upon wages, raw materials and other costs of production. This *surplus value* can then be used by capitalists for personal consumption and for further capital accumulation. It is at this stage in the development of the capitalist mode of production that objective class relations are clearly visible and relatively uncomplicated since the producers undertake their work tasks under the *personal* control and supervision of capitalists. In the *rational* pursuit of profit, capitalists attempt to obtain the *maximum* level of production for the *minimum* of outlay on wages and other costs. There is, then, the emergence of an employment relationship and a capitalist-owned productive process, which is essentially antagonistic and exploitative.

These conditions are favourable for the development of modern industry (Marx, 1974), which is described as such by Marx because of the ways in which the nature of the capitalist mode of production becomes altered by the widespread adoption of machinery. This brings about the creation of highly integrated productive processes in which work tasks are fragmented and made simple. If, during the stage of manufacture, producers use tools for the performance of all-round tasks, under the conditions of modern industry producers become mere appendages to machines. Although skilled workers are needed to maintain and repair equipment, the general drift of technical change is for most tasks to become routinized and de-skilled. Increasingly, there is a technically based division of labour, with machines dictating the pace and pattern of work tasks. Capitalists, through their ownership of the means of production, are able to intensify their control over productive workers. The subordination of labour to capital is reinforced since employees no longer possess skills or earning capabilities that can be used independently from their employers' technology. They are integral members of a labour process, the character of which is determined by the capitalist motive of *rational* capital accumulation.

Although the stage of modern industry, in creating centralized factory-based forms of production, encourages the development of class relations, the visibility of these in many working settings is disguised. This is partly because capitalists' control of the work process is exercised through 'impersonal' machinery and techno-logical processes. But equally, an increase in the scale of productive forces compels employers to delegate many of their supervisory functions. Bureaucratic procedures evolve, so that managers and technical specialists become responsible for coordinating and controlling the work process in a manner that was previously undertaken *personally* by capitalists themselves. The bureaucra-tization of the capitalists' control functions serves to conceal the more visible features of class antagonism. The essentially dichot-omous nature of class relations becomes hidden and accommodated within the hierarchical gradations of authority relations, which thus serve to limit the subjective understanding of class exploitation. Equally, the rational pursuit of profit leads to the growth of large capitalist-owned corporations and hence to the need for greater financial funding than can be provided by single capitalists on their own. The emergence of the joint-stock company, with its limited liability, brings about changes in the form of capitalist ownership. Companies become owned by a number of individuals rather than by single founder-owners, with the effect that producers' percep-tions of the essentially exploitative and class nature of the employ-ment relationship are further inhibited.

Marx, then, identifies distinct and separate stages in the develop-ment of the capitalist mode of production. From these it is evident how changes in the technical forces associated with processes of capital accumulation bring about changes in the nature of employ-ment relations. Forces associated with the rational pursuit of profit through the production and sale of commodities in the market-place lead to the concentration in factories of workers, who become subject to the control of employers, either *directly* through face-to-face relationships or *indirectly* through the use of technical pro-cesses and the delegated authority bestowed in managers and other specialists. Whichever, the generation of economic surpluses for profit is dependent upon an essentially exploitative relationship. Without such exploitation, there can be no profits, no longer-term capital accumulation and, accordingly, no capitalist mode of pro-duction. Hence, whenever the profit motive and the capitalist mode of production are present, there must be social classes. Capitalism cannot sustain itself as a reproductive socio-economic process without there being social classes. They are, in other words, an inherent and indispensable feature of capitalism (Braverman, 1974). This is irrespective of the attitudes and behaviour of those who, whether as capitalists or as workers, undertake various functions within this process. Thus the presence or not of class awareness has no bearing upon whether or not social classes *exist*. The United States, for example, as a capitalist society is character-ized by objective class relations despite the overwhelming accept-ance of values which emphasize the 'individualism' and the 'personal freedoms' of that country (Wright *et al.*, 1982).

What of occupational structures, stratification systems and patterns of socio-economic inequality? Are they, in any way, related to class relationships? Is it possible to describe, for example, patterns of socio-economic inequality without recourse to the analysis of social class? No such description or understanding will be complete unless it is recognized that, under capitalism, occu-pational structures and stratification systems are the manifestation of class relations as rooted within different material and industrial orders. How, then, are these determined under the conditions of contemporary capitalism?

By definition, the essential generic feature of capitalism is the production of goods and services for profit. Some of this profit is then used for re-investment, in order to produce further commodi-ties for further profit. In other words, the whole process is one of rational capital accumulation whereby money is invested in pro-ductive capacity for the production and sale of commodities in the market-place, the proceeds of which are realized, again as money, for the purposes of renewed capital investment. The goods and services so produced must always possess an exchange or market value that is greater than the value of the raw materials and the total costs incurred in production. Since the cost of labour constitutes a proportion of these, it is evident that producers can never be paid the full value of the commodities they produce. Instead, this is expropriated by capitalist enterprises as profit and becomes private property. The owners, then, whether they are individual or institutional shareholders, get a return on their initial investment that has been obtained from the labour of others. Concurrently, the producers never receive the full benefit of the value of the commodities they have provided (Marx, 1974). If they did, there would be no profits and, although capitalist enterprises might be able to sustain themselves for a period of time, ultimately they would be threatened with bankruptcy. Profits, then, are the outcome of a process of expropriation and producers must be *exploited* if the accumulation process is to proceed. Re-investment is also central to the whole process since the forces of production have to be continuously renewed. Capitalist enterprises have to innovate technologically if they are to remain cost-effective and competitive. Since there is a limit to the length of the working day, economic surpluses and profits can only be enhanced through productivity increases made possible by mechanization. It is in these terms that developments in technological change can be understood; the motives underlying the shift to automation and the replacement of human labour by machinery are those of cost-effectiveness, reliability of output and increased productivity. Because of this, technologists, engineers and other technical specialists fulfil important roles within the process of capital accumulation. They have become even more important as corporations have become increasingly capital-intensive and heavily dependent upon technological change for competing in product markets (Davis and Scase, 1985).

This process cannot function without the availability of free labour, a feature that is not found in other modes of production. Under capitalism, workers are free to sell their labour as a commodity in exchange for wages. But capitalists will only purchase this labour as long as it creates value and, therefore, profits. Accordingly, wage labourers can only obtain their means of subsistence through the employment relationship. But once negotiated into this relationship, they become the 'property' of the capitalist, as a means of production necessary for the generation of surplus value. Hence, producers are only *formally* free – that is to say, free to sell their labour power – since without employment they have no means of subsistence. Any skills they do possess are of value only when used with capitalist-owned technology and equipment. Without access to these, their competences have few value-creation properties (Braverman, 1974).

These are the essential features of the capitalist mode of production. It is an accumulation process based upon the production of commodities for sale in the market. It consists of relationships of expropriation whereby the values created by producers

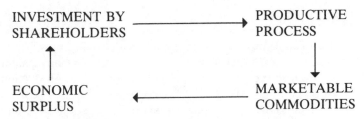

Figure 1 The process of the capitalist mode of production.

become the private property of those who own and control the means of production. The process is summarized in Figure 1.

Investment and profit or, in other words, return on capital invested is at the core of the dynamics of capitalism. Without this, the process cannot operate. Investment, whether it is undertaken by individual owner-managers, as in the case of nineteenth-century entrepreneurs, or by large financial institutions, will take place only if it is *perceived* to be capable of generating 'satisfactory' returns; that is, by comparison with other available investment opportunities (Ingham, 1984). If profits, and thereby returns, on capital invested decline relative to other available possibilities, there will be no incentive to invest. Such declines can be associated with a number of factors, including entry of new competitors into the market and increased operating costs associated with wage labour demands. It is in terms of the latter that the antagonisms of capitalist production relations are most evident. As a cost of production, the price of labour has direct effects upon profits. Hence there is a need for management to *control* labour so that shareholders can receive what they perceive to be a satisfactory return on their investment.

Of course, not all of the economic surplus becomes re-invested in capital growth. Some of it will be distributed in the form of dividends to shareholders while a further proportion is often paid in the form of taxes. Shareholders not only expect the value of their stockholdings to increase through a process of re-investment in the accumulation process, they also often require more immediate financial returns. For individual investors this can be for purposes of consumption, while institutional investors, such as pension funds, trusts and insurance companies, have to meet the

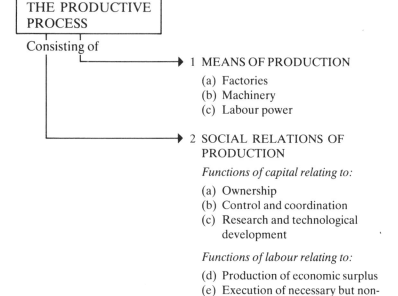

Figure 2   Relations in the productive process.
Source: Davis and Scase (1985)

expectations of satisfactory returns from their own investors. Accordingly, managers of capitalist corporations are compelled to satisfy their shareholders in terms of both capital appreciation and dividend payment. There can often be a 'trade-off' between these demands because profits distributed as dividends cannot be used for re-investment and further capital growth. Often, the objectives of management can be in conflict with those of shareholders because re-investment for business growth can provide opportunities for further career development and the extension of managerial responsibilities. Even so, managerial and shareholder goals are usually united in their joint opposition to the interests of wage earners, whose labour power constitutes a cost of production.

It is in these terms that discussions of social class make sense. What, then, are the linkages between social class, stratification and occupational orders? These relationships can be determined by a more detailed analysis of the capitalist production process as summarized in Figure 2.

In addition to the technical means of production, any capitalist corporation possesses social relations, made up of occupational positions consisting of different duties, responsibilities and demands of accountability. These are dependent upon each other through the structuring of control relationships, whereby those in positions of authority determine the duties of others (Weber, 1968). Even though these may be hierarchically arranged, it is possible to identify the underlying dichotomous and antagonistic nature of employment relationships (Salaman, 1981). Some tasks are associated with the functions of *capital* while others relate to the activities of *labour* (Braverman, 1974). Any profit-making corporation consists of class relationships because of the presence of these features. While those occupying the former positions are, in one way or another, engaged in the expropriation of economic surpluses, those in the latter category are associated with the production of such surpluses. Although this division is less than evident in most profit-making corporations, it is often visible in their day-to-day activities through the structuring of *control* relations. Hence, there are some who are bestowed with responsibilities for enhancing the value of capital investment through their exercise of a variety of managerial, technical and professional competences, while there are others whose labour is 'costed' as a factor of production and who are subordinated to the control of others.

The prime beneficiaries of capitalist corporations are, of course, the owners. They possess the means of production as private property which is protected by state-enforced laws and regulations. Their primary objective, as shareholders, is to enhance the value of their corporate ownership through the accumulation process (Scott, 1985). But they may or may not play an active role in the management of corporations. They could, for example, be non-executive directors whose prime task is to approve corporate policy as presented to them by their executive colleagues at company board meetings. They may not be individual shareholders at all but the representatives of institutional investors. Indeed, the pattern during the twentieth century has been for financial institutions to become the major shareholders of large corporations (Ingham,

1984). Although this trend has weakened the direct and visible relationship between corporate ownership and control, the links remain close through their shared interest in the accumulation process. At an earlier stage of capitalism, as in nineteenth-century Britain, the functions of ownership and control were vested in the hands of entrepreneurs or owner-managers who personally directed the day-to-day activities of their enterprises (Bendix, 1956). With the growth of large-scale corporations, brought about predominantly through mergers and acquisitions, institutional shareholders – represented by non-executive directors – have tended to delegate the functions of corporate management to professionally trained experts. But despite this division of function both parties share a common interest in the rational pursuit of profit. In fact, the modern corporation is usually compelled to be more rational and cost-effective in its profit-making goals than its owner-managed counterpart (Mills, 1951). This is mainly because financial institutions have to optimize their returns on investment to achieve their own performance goals. Insurance companies, occupational pension funds and investment trusts have their own beneficiaries whose expectations for profit have to be met.

In terms of class analysis, the changing composition of corporate ownership, in the form of institutional rather than individual investors who may or may not be directly involved in day-to-day corporate management, has tended to disguise the ownership function to the extent that it is often alleged that the personal ownership of capital has evaporated. However, this is not the case. There continue to be people who are prime beneficiaries either *directly* as individual shareholders or *indirectly* through personal claims on the profits of investing financial institutions. But if the ownership function is less evident, the delegated managerial responsibilities derived from this are far more visible. This is expressed in the day-to-day activities of those who coordinate and control work processes (Anthony, 1986). The growth of large-scale corporations has brought about an increasing need for managerial skills of one kind or another. In small organizations these can often be undertaken by owner-managers but in larger enterprises the rational pursuit of profit through the cost-effective use of the means of production has led to the bureaucratization of decision-making processes, within which specialist managerial tasks are delineated

(Scase and Goffee, 1989). Consequently, the control dimensions of management are less dichotomous than within the nineteenth-century owner-managed business. It is only in large manufacturing companies, where there is often a sharp distinction between 'management' and 'workers', that objective class divisions will be subjectively experienced in pronounced ways (Beynon, 1980). Even so, such class relationships do exist in all profit-making organizations since without management, hierarchically arranged and allocated to different specialists, the production of goods and services for profit could not be rationally pursued. Hence, although corporate managers are employees, they pursue the interests of capital through their supervision and control of the work process. Without the performance of this function, there would be no capital accumulation (Edwards, 1979; de Vroey 1980; Marglin, 1980).

For similar reasons, those engaged in product research, development and planning may be regarded as integral to the ownership function. Although, as with the majority of managers, they may not personally be shareholders, they are employed so that the technical means of production can be continuously modernized, repaired and renovated so that the rational pursuit of profit can be maintained. The highly competitive nature of present-day markets requires the ongoing modernization of production through technological change as well as through the replacement of human labour with highly automated equipment. Technologists, scientists, engineers and various specialists are employed to search out avenues for product development and for cost-effective production systems. In a similar manner to managers, they serve the interests of shareholders in their pursuit of profits and through their predisposition to regard wage labour as a productive cost that must be offset against corporate revenues. Even though they receive wages or salaries, so that many of them may see themselves as 'working-class' because they 'work for a living', the primary nature of their work tasks attaches them to the ownership function. As 'intellectual' employees, they are compelled to utilize their talents and skills for the interests of institutional and/or individual shareholders (Abercrombie and Urry, 1983). It is this shared interest which gives those employees who perform a variety of managerial, technical and professional tasks a common *objective* class position. This is irrespective of their own subjective beliefs and the extent to which there may be disputes between them about the allocation of corporate resources during the course of their day-to-day work activities. Hence, it is useful to make a distinction between the tasks of *strategic* and *operational* management. An undue focus upon the latter can lead observers to argue that there are fundamental sources of division among corporate managers and technical experts. If, however, attention is directed to their *strategic* functions, it is evident that any conflicts that can arise among them are secondary to the overriding goal of profit-making and capital accumulation. Equally, the hierarchical and fragmented nature of management, as it becomes structured within various organizational settings, should not conceal this fundamental objective. In the final analysis, managers share a common *class* interest through their coordination and control of the means of production for the purposes of capital accumulation. As part of this task, they are responsible for the supervision of labour.

According to Marx, labour power is the source of value creation, since without it raw materials cannot be converted into marketable commodities. Thus, in the process of value creation, labour power *must* be exploited in the sense that producers can never get paid for what they earn. If they did, no economic surpluses would be derived from the productive process and there would be no capital accumulation. Hence, those who are exploited in this process are undertaking the functions of labour and as such they too constitute a social class. There are those who perform a variety of necessary but *non-productive* activities while there are others whose labour power is directly and explicitly associated with the production of goods and services for profit. Technological changes have reduced the need for productive manual workers, because of the increasingly capital-intensive nature of modern manufacturing systems (Child, 1988; Jones, 1989). Instead, there is an increasing need for those who are able to provide a range of 'ancillary' or 'support' services. These providers are not directly productive in the sense that their labour does not create surplus value but, even so, they are indispensable in the accumulation process. But why should they be considered as performing tasks of labour rather than of capital, since they do exercise degrees of control? Indeed, some observers have suggested that technical workers, because of their expert skills, occupy an ambiguous or even contradictory class position (Wright, 1976).

However, it would seem justifiable to consider them as working class as a result of the conditions under which they perform their tasks. Although they may enjoy a certain degree of working autonomy, the discretion and judgement they exercise are circumscribed by managers and higher-grade technical professionals. As such, they are controlled by others, with their performance monitored, and they are generally treated as a cost of production. Despite their often higher wages, and better working conditions compared with manual workers, they are excluded from participation within the ownership function. They may be consulted on a day-to-day basis about *operational* matters and be engaged in various decision-making activities, but they are not involved in *strategic* management – certainly not in terms of the formulation of corporate policies, the setting of objectives and the determination of monitoring systems for measuring the output and performance of others. It is by virtue of their exclusion from these strategic decision-making processes that technical, maintenance and 'support' staff, subject as they are to the control of others and costed as a factor of production, constitute a necessary, albeit non-productive, function of labour. They are, then, part of the working class in terms of their location within the social relations of production.

These employees are far less numerous than the routine white-collar workers who make up the great proportion of those who perform necessary but unproductive labour tasks. It is the rapid expansion of these administrative jobs that has led many observers to argue for a 'new' middle class (Hamilton and Hirszowicz, 1987). In this light, they are seen to be performing tasks that require the exercise of judgement and discretion. Although this may be the case in smaller enterprises where various managerial functions are delegated by owner-managers, it is generally not the case for those employed in large-scale organizations who are normally expected to perform routine and relatively non-skilled tasks (Crompton and Jones, 1984). They exercise little authority and they are generally excluded from aspects of both strategic and operational management. Instead, they are compelled to execute instructions and, hence, they are subject to the supervision and control of others. Indeed, large numbers of their jobs have become so 'de-skilled' and routinized that they have been taken over by new technology (Crompton and Reid, 1982; Baran, 1988). The jobs that remain tend to be undertaken by those whose labour power can be purchased cheaply: school-leavers and married women who are often prepared or forced to offer their services on a part-time basis. Such employees usually lack security of employment and the fringe benefits that are enjoyed by managerial, professional and higher-grade technical staff. Although their physical working conditions may be better than those experienced by factory workers, they enjoy few, if any, other advantages (Cockburn, 1986). It is for these reasons that routine white-collar employees may be seen as undertaking the functions of labour. Although they may be non-productive, their tasks are necessary within the overall process of capital accumulation. They perform their tasks under the supervision and control of others and in ways that are similar to those encountered by other members of the working class.

The social relations of production, then, consist of functions relating to ownership and functions associated with labour. The owners are concerned with the exercise of authority and control, while labour is compelled, through these same control relation-ships, to undertake various productive and non-productive but necessary work tasks. In itself, of course, the exercise of control is of no importance; it only has relevance when it is utilized for particular objectives. In capitalist enterprises these are the production and realization of surplus values as expressed in the profit motive and the imperative of capital accumulation. Capitalist control relation-ships may be hierarchically arranged and diffused among a number of managerial, professional and technical specialists but these are united in their strategic objectives. It is this that legitimates their day-to-day operational activities, and in their pursuit of the goals of capital accumulation they exploit the labour of others for the execution of non-productive and productive work tasks. The functions of capital and labour are interdependent and, accord-ingly, the class relations of capitalist corporations are *both* antagon-istic and cooperative. Management has a vested interest in emphasizing the cooperative or 'harmonious' nature of manager–worker relations since this can inhibit the development of class awareness (Wickens, 1987). But perhaps more importantly, em-ployees do not normally perceive themselves as performing the functions of either labour or capital. Instead, they regard them-selves as undertaking particular jobs in which there are vested various degrees of responsibility and authority. Employees fulfil occupational roles and, although these are *derived* from the social relations of production and hence are part-and-parcel of class relationships, it is their occupations that constitute the basis for self-identity and personal esteem as well as for any feelings of social justice and equity. It is because of this that occupational interests are more evident than class interests in everyday life, with the latter usually considered to be irrelevant (Newby *et al.*, 1985). However, before this issue can be discussed further, it is necessary to consider whether this analysis of class is only applicable for understanding social relations of large-scale, productive manufacturing corporations. Since these are a declining source of employment in Western capitalist countries, it could be argued that Marxist-based models of social class are of diminishing utility.

Many observers claim this. They suggest that the production of goods is now undertaken through the use of capital-intensive, automated processes that dramatically reduce the need for wage labourers of the sort that Marx described in his analysis of capitalism. There is less need for productive labourers but an increasing demand for those engaged in the *realization* process; that is, for those involved in the distribution and retailing of commodities in the market. There are, then, substantial sectors of the occupational structure that are removed from the production process and hence seem inappropriate for analysis according to Marxist-based concepts of class (Hamilton and Hirszowicz, 1987). On closer scrutiny this is not necessarily the case. This can be seen by considering occupations associated with the realization process as found within the spheres of distribution, retail and consumption, as well as those that are even more removed from the profit-making process in that they are located in state-owned institutions concerned with the provision of such services as health, education and welfare.

Corporations engaged in the sale and distribution of goods and services, in common with value-creating manufacturing enterprises, have profit-making and longer-term capital accumulation as their predominant goals. Hence, they have individual and institutional shareholders who are the chief beneficiaries of the profit-making process. Carrying out this function are those with delegated responsibilities for strategic management and others concerned with supervising day-to-day activities through coordinating and controlling the behaviour of those who are compelled to undertake, under instructions, various routine tasks. To take an example, an insurance company will have shareholders who are the beneficiary owners; senior managers who determine corporate strategies for achieving profit-making goals; middle and junior managers who are responsible for the day-to-day coordination and control of those who sell insurance policies to customers; and others who undertake necessary, but routine, clerical and administrative tasks. The latter categories, in an analogous way to workers in profit-making industrial organizations, undertake the functions of labour (Braverman, 1974; Crompton and Jones, 1984). In a similar fashion, it is possible to analyse the social relations of such diverse corporations as large retail stores, advertising agencies, banks and other financial institutions, leisure, recreation and entertainment companies and other profit-making, non-manufacturing organizations. In other words, service sector businesses have comparable social relations and, therefore, social classes of the sort that Marx described for manufacturing enterprises. On a day-to-day basis these are expressed as control relationships, with those exercising the function of ownership controlling the behaviour of others who are forced to execute the sale or administration of goods and services according to routine and, often, highly bureaucratized procedures (Salaman, 1981). Occupational positions within these organizations, therefore, can be allocated to social classes according to their location within these control relations.

In an analogous fashion, class positions can be determined within non-profit-making state-owned institutions. Although they are removed from the value-creation or realization activities of capitalist corporations – even though such state institutions may serve the 'needs' of capital through their 'production' of educated and healthy employees – they do, in a similar fashion to profit-making corporations, have control relations. Again, there are positions responsible for determining organizational strategies and goals, others associated with day-to-day supervision and control, and others that undertake the execution of routine non-manual and manual tasks. In any state-owned hospital, school or welfare agency, as in any profit-making factory, there are those who exercise commands over others, who are expected to execute their tasks according to prescribed rules and procedures. Equally, those who issue the commands and exercise control over the work process are better paid and enjoy favourable working conditions and good fringe benefits. It is, then, *by analogy*, possible to determine class relations and class positions within organizations that are removed from the productive process. This is not surprising given the fact that state-owned institutions are usually deliberately structured to imitate the control relationships of profit-making corporations. They have, inherent within them, similar assumptions about managerial prerogatives and the structuring of work relations. Accordingly, they are organized according to similar principles of control so that the absence of a profit motive need make little difference. There may not be an expropriation of surplus values, but the organization and control of work remain very similar (Scase and Goffee, 1989).

In this chapter it has been argued that social class and class relations continue to be relevant features of present-day capitalist society. Within profit-making corporations it is possible to determine the functions of capital and labour as these are associated with the production and exportation of surplus values. The antagonistic nature of this relationship generates social classes that are characterized by differences in their claims on economic rewards and employment conditions. Most importantly, these class relations express themselves as control relationships; especially between those who are responsible for strategic decision-making and others who are subordinated and tightly controlled in the performance of their work tasks. Similar relationships prevail within corporations engaged in the realization rather than the production of surplus values. Equally, they are found in non-capitalist or state-owned, non-profit-making institutions in which no surplus values are produced. For this reason it can be argued that all who are engaged in the occupational order must inevitably fill class positions. However, at the beginning of this chapter, the present-day relevance of class was queried because most people do not generally perceive themselves, or others, in class terms. But irrespective of these perceptions, organizations and, hence, capitalist societies are structured according to social classes if only because of the character of their social relations. How, then, can these objectively structured social classes be seen to be relevant to the understanding of attitudes, behaviour and personal life-styles? This is a link that has to be established; it can be determined by designating the connections that exist between social classes and occupational positions.

In many analyses, social classes are constructed *out of* occupational groupings (Marshall *et al.*, 1988). In other words, different occupations are aggregated into 'class' categories of the sort found in the Registrar General's description of social classes in Britain. Research investigations also normally ask respondents 'what do you do?' and, on the basis of elicited job titles and rudimentary job descriptions, occupational titles are determined and then allocated to class categories. However, logically, the 'reverse' procedure is more appropriate since the nature of occupations is determined by the class relations of modern organizations.

There is a widely held assumption that jobs and occupations constitute relatively stable and precisely defined work activities which are determined by the 'objective' requirements of administrative and technological work systems (Bell, 1973). Accordingly, jobs are delineated according to their technical, skill or specialist functions, and are seen to exist 'independently' of workplace social relations. However, work tasks and, hence, occupations and jobs are also designated according to their duties, authority and responsibilities. They have built into them assumptions about legitimate control over technical, financial and human resources (Weber, 1968). Thus, occupations within organizations, irrespective of whether or not they are profit-making capitalist enterprises, are shaped by the structuring of control relations determined by those who exercise the greatest authority; namely, those who undertake the functions of delegated ownership, such as directors and senior managers. Equally, managers responsible for day-to-day operational activities exercise control through the authority delegated to them. Hence, the imperative need for management is that the activities of staff have to be *coordinated* and *controlled* since without this little would be achieved in the form of cost-effectiveness, productivity and profits (Dahrendorf, 1959). In other words, the social relations of production consist of control relationships and it is these that determine the tasks, duties and responsibilities of different jobs. Thus, jobs and occupations are the *outcome* of class relations and they can be directly related to the functions of ownership and of labour, as outlined in Figure 3.

SOCIAL RELATIONS OF PRODUCTION $\rightarrow$	CLASS STRUCTURE $\rightarrow$	OCCUPATIONAL CATEGORIES
Functions of capital relating to:		
(a) Ownership		(a) Shareholders and proprietors
(b) Control and coordination	Middle class	(b) Directors, managers, higher-grade professional employees
(c) Research and technological development		(c) Scientists, engineers and technologists
Functions of labour relating to:		
(d) Production of economic surplus	Working class	(d) Productive manual workers
(e) Execution of necessary but non-productive tasks		(e) clerical, secretarial, routine 'non-manual', 'support' and maintenance workers

Figure 3 Functions of capital and labour, class and occupational categories.

Figure 3 refers to the 'pure type' of capitalist enterprise where profits and capital accumulation are pursued through the production of goods and services for sale in the market. Its purpose is to outline the way in which different occupational categories are derived from the social relations of production. By the nature of their different functions these occupations are the expression of class relations of the kind described by Marx, and the occupational order is an outcome of these class relations. Hence, occupations do not determine the nature of social classes; instead, it is class relations, embedded as these are within the control relationships of organizations, that determine the delineation of occupations and, therefore, occupational orders.

From the preceding discussion it is clear that the study of social classes and their changing dynamic must remain central to sociological analysis. It is only by reference to class, as determined by the social relations of economic and social organizations, that it is possible to understand the changing composition of occupational orders and, related to these, patterns of privilege and disadvantage. But having said that, it must be conceded that for the great majority of employees it will be their jobs and occupations rather than their social class membership that will determine the core elements of their personal identities. Such employees are unlikely to appreciate how the essential dynamics of class shape the content and parameters of their jobs and, more importantly, the control that they exercise (or not) over others. There is no reason why they should, since for most purposes employees' self-interests can be better pursued through various occupational rather than class-based strategies. This is the dilemma of those concerned with political mobilization, because of their inability to heighten the level of class consciousness among those engaged in different jobs and occupations (Lockwood, 1988). But this is hardly surprising in view of the ways in which payment systems, notions of personal esteem and self-respect, and even strategies for collective action, are organized around occupational groupings rather than social class. Even so, the general lack of understanding about the significance of class relations as they are structured within organizations does not deny their continuing importance. It is the task of academic sociologists to describe and explain this dynamic and how it is the determining factor in the process of profit-making and capital accumulation. However, for detailed analyses of attitudes and behaviour, of reward systems, of life-styles and of life chances, the focus of enquiry will continue to be occupational groupings; even though these must inevitably be viewed as expressions of class relations, located as they are within the structures of organizations. Thus, the next chapter focuses upon the ways in which occupations, shaped by the social relations of both profit-making and non-profit-making organizations, are differently rewarded to produce class-based stratification systems.

2

Class and Stratification: Patterns of Rewards

Concepts of social stratification are frequently confused with social class and, indeed, the two are often considered as interchangeable (Davis and Moore, 1945). In view of our definition of social class, however, one is cause and the other effect. Stratification systems in capitalist society are the expression of class relations and reflect the ways in which class creates structured economic inequalities. As stated in Chapter 1, the production and expropriation of economic surpluses are undertaken according to relations of control and it would be surprising if these did not express themselves in the *distribution* of resources. But just as class and class relations are 'hidden' within the productive process so too are they hidden within the spheres of distribution and personal consumption. Just as occupational orders make up the empirically visible features of capitalist production, they also constitute the daily reality of stratification systems. Hence, occupations tend to be hierarchically arranged in their claims on economic resources, access to privileges of various sorts, and forms of social prestige and honour (Halsey, 1986). Stratification systems reflect the control relations that constitute the core elements of class structures.

The stratification of Western capitalist countries tend to be similar in the ways in which occupations are differentially rewarded (Esping-Andersen, 1990). Reflecting class relations, managerial and professional occupations are generally more highly rewarded than others. In different countries a similar hierarchical pattern persists:

- owner-managers of large enterprises and individuals with substantial property assets and shareholdings;

- directors, managers and higher grade professional and technical employees;
- lower grade professional, managerial and technical employees, and owner-managers of medium and small enterprises;
- skilled and semi-skilled manual, clerical, secretarial and routine non-manual employees;
- unskilled manual employees and those who participate 'part-time' in the labour market.

The cross-national consistency of this pattern, together with its relative long-term stability, is indicative of how occupational groupings associated with the functions of capital, through their exercise of control over work processes, are able to allocate to themselves a favourable share of the available economic resources in the form of salaries, fringe benefits, pensions, performance-related remuneration packages and, increasingly, share options. Such rewards are legitimated as constituting necessary 'costs', *after* which any economic surpluses, profits and returns on capital invested by shareholders are calculated. The wages and earnings of manual and routine non-manual employees are also considered as costs but these are perceived by senior managers as a charge against profits and, therefore, always subject to close control. In other words, the latter are always regarded by corporate leaders as potentially *reducible* costs as distinct from the *fixed* and more permanent costs of their own rewards. Thus, the more advantaged rewards of managerial and professional occupations are structured within profit and loss accountancy procedures as fixed costs and, as such are viewed as a permanent charge on corporations' trading activities. Hence, their remuneration is not subject to the same degree of scrutiny as that of the employees over whom they exercise control. What criteria, then, determine the precise character of earnings differentials? Why should inequalities within capitalist corporations be as they are rather than of a greater or lesser magnitude? Such inequalities appear to be the result of at least four factors.

The first is 'custom and practice'. There tends to be a general acceptance among employees that senior managers and others responsible for the control of the economic process *should* be more highly rewarded than others (Pahl, 1984). This assumption requires, for the purposes of legitimacy, little in the form of explanation simply because employees regard existing inequalities as an inevitable feature of the objective reality of work. Second, if any explanations for existing inequalities are required, they tend to be lodged in arguments about *incentives*. Hence, it is argued that the reward systems of organizations are inevitably unequal, since otherwise there would be no motivation for individuals to want to occupy positions of responsibility and control (Parkin, 1971). Without incentives, corporate efficiency will be impaired since there will cease to be the development of competences necessary for filling senior management positions. This argument impinges upon the third explanation for the existence of inequalities; namely, they are *functional* for the very survival of such organizations (Offe, 1976). It is argued according to this 'functional theory' that inequalities are necessary to motivate those with the necessary talent to undergo the costs of training required for appointment to technical, professional and managerial positions (Davis and Moore, 1945). Hence, inequalities are functional for the efficiency of the capitalist dynamic and so are inculcated within the value systems of society as a whole. Finally, wage differentials reflect the bargaining capacity of different occupational groups (Gilbert, 1986). As mentioned above, senior managers and corporate leaders rarely have to bargain over their salaries because they enjoy considerable autonomy in the capacity to determine their own rewards. But the ability of others to obtain rewards is largely dependent upon their bargaining power and how they are able to use this to obtain concessions from senior managers. This bargaining capacity will be shaped by a variety of factors. Of these, the indispensability of particular skills will be paramount, although often precarious. Managers can often introduce new forms of technology that will either render skills redundant or bring about processes of 'de-skilling' so that the tasks can be undertaken by 'dispensable' employees (Sabel, 1982). Alternatively, complete work processes can be relocated to where labour is cheaper and more compliant with management (Murray, 1988). Indeed, during the 1980s management was particularly active in introducing forms of technology and work processes that rendered obsolete the 'indispensable' skills of their employees. However, the bargaining capacity of occupational groupings is also shaped by broader market forces, which determine the supply and demand for their skills. Compared with earlier decades, there is now little need for craft workers in most European countries. On the other hand, the demand for those with computer, scientific and technological competences has increased considerably. Hence, management-sponsored technological change helps to shape these forces, changing the labour needs of corporations.

There are, then, various reasons for inequalities in occupational earnings. Through conventional assumptions and expectations about income differentials, these inequalities become resistant to change. Thus wage increases offered to low-paid employees rarely reduce inequalities because similar increases are then granted to higher earners in order that corporate incentive systems remain undisturbed. More broadly, therefore, overall patterns of inequality within society tend not to change. Generally, arguments that have been put forward to account for cross-national similarities have emphasized the functional imperatives of modern technology and the inherent 'logic' of industrial systems (Kerr *et al.*, 1960). However, such approaches are often unclear as to how technological or industrial processes, in themselves, can *determine* structures of inequality and bring about similarities between countries. They tend to ignore the class character of productive processes and how occupations are structured within class relations. If similarities within the stratification systems of different countries are to be explained, it is necessary to analyse the nature of their class structures and how these are articulated within the social relations of production. The development of capitalism in different Western countries has produced similar patterns, in the expression of both class relations and stratification systems (Davis and Scase, 1985). Any differences between countries are but variations on a common theme. But in considering patterns of inequality and, hence, systems of social stratification, it is useful to focus upon three core components: ownership, wage and salary differentials, and the distribution of income, as reflected in the economic rewards of non-earners as well as earners.

Many discussions of stratification neglect patterns of ownership. They therefore produce an incomplete picture of economic rewards, particularly as these are shaped by the dynamic of class relations. Analyses such as these are characterized by at least two weaknesses. First, patterns of inequality become conflated because income derived from sources other than wage and salary earnings are neglected. Receipts from dividends and capital growth derived from share ownership are discounted. Second, the nature of the ownership function, which is central to the dynamic of capitalism, the accumulation process and the expropriation of the economic surplus, is overlooked. Accordingly, more complete analyses of stratification systems have to consider the role of ownership, since without this they cannot establish the overall relationship that exists between patterns of stratification and class structures. In Britain, for instance, the accumulation process has sustained, and continues to sustain, a concentrated group of owners who have been able to pass down their personal wealth to their offspring through generations (Scott, 1985). The ownership they exercise within the production process enables them to enjoy privileged patterns of consumption, despite broader socio-political changes. For instance, the growth of the welfare state and the development of an organized labour movement have failed to dilute the concentration of capital ownership. Equally, recurrent 'crises' in the British economy and more recent processes of de-industrialization and economic restructuring have had little effect upon the ownership of the rich and the overall distribution of ownership and wealth. Indeed, the rich appear to be remarkably astute in their ability to control the accumulation process for their own benefit (Pond, 1989). This is confirmed by the figures in Table 2.1, which summarizes features of the distribution of personal wealth in Britain in the 1970s and early 1980s.

While there may have been some decline in the share of the wealth possessed by the top 1 per cent, the rest of the top 5 per cent have been able to retain their proportion over this period. In 1985, the top 25 per cent owned 76 per cent of all personal wealth and the top 50 per cent no less than 93 per cent. If there has been any redistribution, it has been *within* the rich rather than between this and other groups. Any shifts that have occurred within this wealthy group can be largely explained by three factors. First, because of their various fiscal skills, their sons and daughters have legal title to assets, so that they avoid such measures as capital transfer tax and death duties. Second, they are able to avoid taxes by setting up

Table 2.1   The distribution of personal wealth in Britain, 1971–1985

	1971	1976	1980	1985
Top 1%	31	24	20	20
Next 4%	21	21	19	20
Next 5%	13	15	13	14
Top 10%	65	60	52	54
Next 15%	21	24	23	22
Top 50%	97	95	94	93

Source: Central Statistical Office (1988)

charitable family trusts and investment funds over which they can exercise personal control. In this way, they are able to absolve themselves of legal title to ownership but, at the same time, retain substantive possession of their personal financial assets. Thus, and in this sense it is necessary to consider families rather than individuals as the relevant financial units, they continue to be the beneficiaries of wealth although, of course, this will not appear as such within statutory statistics on personal ownership. Finally, any reduction in the proportion of the wealth held by the rich during the past two decades appears to have been the result of downturns in financial markets, bringing about a decline in the value of stocks and shares. On the other hand, the appreciation of property prices during the 1980s has probably had the reverse effect and this has almost certainly compensated for any losses that may have occurred as a result of other fiscal and economic changes. The ownership of wealth in Britain, then, has proven to be very resistant to a broad range of economic, political and social changes (Pond, 1989). This reaffirms the extent to which class relations, associated with the ownership and control of the accumulation process, have continued to benefit a very small and privileged group in society. Accordingly, no analysis of the stratification system is complete without taking this into account. But, in doing this, it is also necessary to consider the composition of this ownership and how this is reflected in the legal title to various assets of one kind or another. Some of the more important aspects are presented in Table 2.2.

Table 2.2 The distribution of personal assets in Britain, 1982

	Proportion of each type of asset owned by			
	Top 1%	*Top 2%*	*Top 5%*	*Top 10%*
Minimum amount owned	£190,000	£120,000	£75,000	£50,000
Listed UK company securities	45.6	64.0	78.3	88.4
Unlisted UK company securities	63.8	72.4	80.0	83.5
Cash and bank deposits	8.0	14.8	23.2	35.6
Insurance policies	5.6	11.7	22.3	37.0
Partnership shares	34.0	53.1	40.4	82.0
Land	69.9	80.0	88.0	92.1

Source: Pond (1989)

From Table 2.2 it is evident that roughly nine-tenths of all productive assets, in the form of company stocks and shares and property, are owned by one-tenth of the population. There is a wider spread of ownership of bank deposits and insurance policies but this is hardly surprising. Certainly, the figures suggest that if capitalism was to be more widely owned, as is frequently proposed by the Conservative Party, there would need to be nothing short of a revolution in the composition of capital ownership in Britain. The ability of those who make up the top 10 per cent to retain their ownership and, indeed, to pass it on to their offspring, despite the processes of capital restructuring that have occurred in post-war Britain, is remarkable. It confirms the extent to which relations of ownership and control are mutually reinforcing within the class structure and able to resist the egalitarian demands of organized labour. Despite the growth of trade unionism and the election to office of Labour governments, the class control exercised by the rich has remained largely unchallenged. This extremely privileged group can justifiably be regarded as a ruling class because of its capacity, through the ownership and control of the productive process, to expropriate a disproportionate share of the economic surplus.

This is not to deny that there have been changes in the means whereby this ownership has been exercised. It has tended to become less visible during the course of the twentieth century as the scale of capitalist enterprises has expanded through amalgamations and takeovers (Hannah and Kay, 1977). Paradoxically, as corporations have extended their domination over the production and distribution of goods and services, those individuals who benefit through their ownership function have become more concealed from popular scrutiny. Consequently, working-class awareness of the magnitude to which the ownership of wealth is extremely concentrated is very low. This lack of awareness is now being reinforced by attempts to develop popular capitalism through the encouragement of broader patterns of petty ownership (Labour Research, 1987). Through a very limited personal ownership of corporate stocks and shares, a section of the working class is acquiring a material stake in the accumulation process, which serves to legitimate the notion of capitalist ownership in general. But what accounts for the limited awareness of wealth concentration in a country such as Britain?

It has to do with two major processes of change affecting the nature of relationships between the functions of ownership and control. First, there has been an increasing separation of these two functions, with many of the tasks of management performed by those who have little or no stake in the ownership of their employing corporations; certainly by comparison with smaller family-owned firms, owner-managed enterprises and privately owned medium-size companies (Scase and Goffee, 1987). Despite the popularity of small business start-up in the closing decades of the twentieth century, the concentration of ownership over the production process has continued, bringing with it the development of bureaucratized management control systems and the emergence of specialist, professional managers (Scott, 1985). It is they who exercise the control functions on a day-to-day basis, on behalf of shareholders, and class relations in the work place, if they are perceived as such, are experienced in these terms. It is these control relations, rather than ownership, that shape the nature of class awareness. Legal title to ownership is largely seen as irrelevant, while the exercise of control derived from corporate ownership is perceived to be the underlying force of class relations. Hence, the nationalized industries in

Britain, managed with traditional capitalist strategies and methods of control, have generated similar patterns of workplace attitudes and behaviour among employees to those found within privately owned corporations. The state *ownership* of these corporations has been regarded as largely irrelevant and such enterprises could, in Britain in the 1980s, be transferred into forms of private ownership with little or no protest from those employed within them.

Second, the ownership of productive resources is now more veiled than in the past because it is exercised more indirectly. During the post-war era, there has been a change in the nature of corporate shareholdings, from individual to institutional investment (Ingham, 1984). This does not mean that this has fundamentally changed the composition of the major beneficiaries. It is rather that the rich make use of more indirect, institutional means to benefit from the ownership of wealth-creating processes. Their financial assets are in the form of trusts, investment funds and financial institutional holdings, which are invested in profit-making corporations. On the face of it, therefore, the predominant shareholders of large corporations are not individuals but financial institutions that are, themselves, managed on the basis of rational and technical competences. It is this that adds substance to claims that the ownership function of modern capitalism has become institutionalized (Ingham, 1984). But such a view can ignore the prime beneficiaries of this changing process. Granted, there has been a growth of occupational pension funds and an increase in the importance of insurance companies as major shareholders of corporations. But although some of their beneficiaries may be working-class employees, they tend overwhelmingly to be those who are engaged in managerial, professional and senior corporate positions. Thus, such groups benefit from the dynamic of the accumulation process in two ways: first, directly, through their high earnings and related fringe benefits which they receive as employee rewards; second, indirectly, through their participation in the ownership function of corporations by virtue of their claims on pension funds and endowment policies, and their stakes in corporate shareholdings through their participation in investment, unit trusts and managed financial bonds of one kind or another. Indeed, the composition of the ownership of stocks and shares in British companies reflects this shift from *direct* personal to *indirect*

Table 2.3 Ownership of company shares in the United Kingdom

Type of shareholder	Percentage of market value held		
	1963	*1975*	*1989*
Personal	54	38	20
Insurance companies	10	16	20
Pension funds	6	17	32
Unit trusts	1	4	8
Investment trusts	10	10	
Other	19	15	20
Total	100	100	100

Source: Scott (1985), Confederation of British Industry (1990)

institutional ownership, as shown in Table 2.3. It must be emphasized, however, that the prime beneficiaries of the wealth-creating, profit-making accumulation process remain a small grouping – the very rich – who, through their investment and fiscal strategies, have been able to maintain and even enhance their economic privileges.

From Table 2.3 it can be seen that the direct personal ownership of shares has declined from more than one-half in the early 1960s to roughly one-third in the 1970s, while the stakes of pension funds and insurance companies have increased considerably. The use of institutional vehicles as modes of investment by the rich gives them a number of benefits. First, they are able to make use of the expert skills of those who work in financial institutions to ensure that the value of their investments is maximized through the use of sophisticated financial analyses, usually on a global scale. Second, they are able to ensure that their investments are mobile and that they can be shifted between profit-making ventures as and when favourable opportunities arise. Further, they can obtain fiscal advantages from using financial institutions as investment vehicles because they are able to minimize the effects of or even circumvent various tax measures. Thus, it can be concluded that despite changes which may have occurred in the legal ownership of the means of production – from individual to institutional shareholders – the prime beneficiaries remain a small number of individuals and families who are able to preserve their economic privileges. Although the growth of institutional forms of corporate investment conceals them, it remains the case that class relations, structured within the productive process, generate economic surpluses which become, disproportionately, the personal wealth of a small number of people. Hence, any analysis of a stratification system that ignores this process is largely incomplete. Studies of social stratification that focus almost exclusively upon occupational wage differentials overlook a major force that accounts for the great concentrations of wealth in modern society. Even so, the occupational order is a core dimension of any system of social stratification.

There have, of course, been considerable changes in the occupational structures of Western capitalist countries. These reflect a number of processes, including changing patterns of managerial control, the implementation of new technological processes, the increasing scale and complexity of profit-making organizations, and broader national and international socio-economic processes that have brought large-scale economic and industrial restructuring in their wake. All of these have affected the nature of work practices and the ways in which occupations are structured within class relations. But perhaps most importantly, the development of capitalist corporations has been characterized by their increasing quasi-monopolistic forms, their technological complexity and their constant need to change work processes because of the changing demands of markets. These corporations have had to become more sophisticated and rational in their managerial practices, in terms of both the *control* and the *coordination* of technical, financial and human resources. Such changes are reflected in the occupational structures of Western capitalist countries, with there being a rapid expansion in the proportion of managerial, professional and technical positions. Equally, the tendency to replace human labour with machinery to make productive processes more rational and cost-effective has led to a decline in the numbers required to perform productive manual tasks. For the United Kingdom, the major trends seem to be as shown in Table 2.4.

Table 2.4 does not fully reflect a number of important trends that have appeared in post-war Britain. Changing patterns of world trade have brought about processes of economic restructuring and these, in turn, have affected the composition of the labour force.

Table 2.4 Distribution of the economically active population by occupational category in the United Kingdom, 1951–1981

Occupational category	1951	1961	1971	1981
Employers and own account	6.7	6.4	6.5	6.4
Managers and administrators	5.4	5.3	8.0	10.1
Professionals and technicians	6.6	9.0	11.1	14.7
Clerical and sales	16.3	18.6	19.5	19.3
Supervisors and foremen	2.6	2.9	3.9	4.2
Skilled manual	23.8	24.1	20.2	16.0
Semi-skilled manual	26.6	25.1	19.3	19.0
Unskilled manual	11.9	8.5	11.6	10.4
Total	99.9	99.9	100.1	100.1

Source: Heath and McDonald (1987); reprinted in Sarre (1989)

Many working-class jobs have become 'de-skilled' while other full-time tasks have been subdivided into part-time positions. It has been argued that 'Fordist' principles of economic production are becoming replaced by more 'flexible' work practices, made possible by the implementation of new technologies, and the growing use of sub-contracting and 'putting out' as ways of producing goods on a more cost-effective basis (Atkinson and Meager, 1985). But certainly none of the changes that have occurred with the occupational structure have brought about the demise of class relations. Nor have they generated greater equalities within the stratification system. Indeed, there seems to be a growing polarization between those performing the functions of capital, that is managerial, professional and higher-grade technical jobs, on the one hand, and those undertaking the tasks of labour on the other (Pond, 1989). This is partly because of the incremental nature of managerial and professional earnings. Such employees tend to start their careers on relatively low salaries, often lower than those obtained by productive manual employees. But during the course of their working lives, they obtain incremental pay rises so that by their late thirties or early forties there are sharp contrasts in patterns of wage differentials (Davis and Scase, 1985). By this age, the high earnings of managerial and professional employees reflect the control functions they exercise over the productive process.

Although rewards are attached to occupational positions, they are received by individuals. It is *people* who experience the deprivations and the privileges that are the outcome of class relations in the productive process. In this, there have been considerable changes in Western capitalist societies during the post-war era – most importantly, the large increase in the numbers of women and members of ethnic minority groups who participate in the labour market (Gallie, 1988). These groups have not been allocated to a broad range of occupational roles. Instead, both women and members of ethnic minorities are concentrated in occupations that are overwhelmingly low-paid and lowly esteemed, and that offer poor career opportunities, working conditions and fringe benefits. A variety of factors account for this, ranging from employer recruitment strategies and prejudice through to the limited technical skills of many women and ethnic minorities because of their disadvantaged educational and training backgrounds. This has led to the suggestion that Western economies have 'dual' or 'fragmented' labour markets within which women and ethnic minorities, in particular, constitute an 'underclass' or, at least, a subordinated and deprived stratum within the working class. Further, it is alleged that white men enjoy a variety of job rewards that are denied to, for example, younger female and ethnic employees. Hence, it is claimed that labour markets can be seen as consisting of 'primary' and 'secondary' sectors, with those in the latter having rather precarious claims on relatively insecure and low paid jobs. However, others do not participate in the labour market and so it is necessary to consider broader patterns of income distribution as a further dimension of social stratification.

Income distributions are more comprehensive measures of inequality – although, of course, they exclude the ownership of wealth – because they incorporate the income received by non-earners, such as pensioners, the unemployed and single parents dependent upon state support. Accordingly, governments can bring about changes in patterns of income distribution through such fiscal measures as the adoption of progressive taxation as well as by providing levels of social benefit that will improve the economic

Table 2.5   Percentage share of income, before and after tax, received by given quantile groups in Britain, 1949–1985

	1949	1959	1979	1985
Before tax				
Top 1%	11.2	8.4	5.3	6.4
Top 10%	33.2	29.4	26.1	29.5
Next 40%	43.1	47.5	50.4	48.3
Bottom 50%	27.3	23.0	23.5	22.2
Bottom 10%	–	–	2.4	2.3
After tax				
Top 1%	6.4	5.3	3.9	4.9
Top 10%	27.1	25.2	23.4	26.5
Next 40%	46.4	49.7	50.4	48.6
Bottom 50%	26.5	25.0	26.2	24.9
Bottom 10%	–	–	2.9	2.7

Source: Pond (1989)

circumstances of those excluded from labour market participation. However, governments seem to have done little through taxation systems to alter the distribution of income among wage earners or through welfare provisions to narrow, in any fundamental way, the broader patterns of income inequality. Indeed, as far as Britain is concerned, there seems to have been a shift towards greater inequality in both pre- and post-tax incomes during the 1980s as shown in Table 2.5.

In the 1980s, the top 10 per cent increased their share of both pre- and post-tax income while the shares accruing to the bottom 50 and 10 per cent declined. A number of processes underlie these trends, including corporate wage strategies, demographic trends producing an ageing, dependent population, government fiscal policies and an increase in the general level of unemployment. But what seems to be equally important in accounting for these increasing inequalities is a set of ideological and structural factors. Ideological factors relating to corporate appeals for enhanced earnings inequalities to provide better incentives for managers, professionals and technical employees undertaking the tasks of coordination and control. Structural factors associated with patterns of occupational change in which work tasks have become de-skilled and broken down into part-time jobs for women and other low-income groups. Hence, the increasing incomes inequalities of the 1980s reflect the changing nature of work tasks as a result of changing managerial and technological processes associated with class relations.

Systems of social stratification, then, are shaped by the dynamics of class relations as these operate within the spheres of production, distribution and consumption. The focus in this chapter has been upon inequalities of income and wealth rather than issues of social honour or prestige. This has been deliberate in view of the fact that, generally, the relative status or honour enjoyed by occupational groupings is derived from their location within class relations. Perhaps somewhat more importantly, however, is the neglect of issues of class mobility and opportunity. If class relations determine the nature of stratification orders in the form of reward systems, equally they shape the structuring of opportunities for personal advancement. This is the topic of the next chapter.

3

Class and Stratification: Patterns of Opportunity

If societies are stratified according to economic rewards, they are similarly divided in patterns of opportunity. Mobility studies are concerned with determining the relative openness of class structures. In this, they tend to focus upon occupations and occupational categories, which are hierarchically arranged within stratification systems according to the rewards they obtain and, related to these, the control they exercise over work processes. These are then used to study one or more of a number of mobility processes. Often a distinction is made between *inter-generational* and *intra-generational* mobility. With the former, the emphasis is upon comparisons between the occupational attainments of children and parents (usually fathers). With the latter, the job histories of individuals are examined to determine the extent to which they have been upwardly or downwardly mobile between occupational groupings. A distinction if often also made between 'elite' and 'mass' mobility, with the former referring to patterns of recruitment into various managerial and professional positions and the latter describing more general processes within the occupational structure as a whole (Heath, 1981). Whichever of these perspectives is adopted, the overall objective of mobility studies is essentially the same: to determine the extent to which the class structures of capitalist societies are open or closed. In other words, although social class may be endemic to the profit-making accumulation process, how far are these structurally determined positions characterized by 'open' or 'closed' patterns of recruitment, and how far are privileges and deprivations inter-generationally transmitted?

Studies of social mobility are rarely perceived by non-sociologists as relevant to the understanding of everyday life. Just like notions of class, social mobility rates mean little to those who are unfamiliar with sociological debate. How, then, can mobility analyses be related to everyday experiences so that they can be perceived as meaningful for the understanding of personal life chances? The link can often be established by relating patterns of social mobility to processes of *recruitment* and *promotion* as these occur within organizations. Instead of emphasizing this dimension, however, sociological studies are inclined to focus upon mobility rates *in society*, with explanations sought in terms of broad social patterns. Such discussions emphasize the importance of educational systems and the extent to which the character of these is related to rates of mobility. Hence, the general shift towards non-streamed comprehensive schooling in different European countries in the 1960s and 1970s is evaluated in terms of its impact upon 'democratizing' opportunities in society. Attempts to broaden the acquisition of credentials by increasing rates of participation in higher education institutions and by developing post-experience education are considered in a similar vein. Accordingly, the expansion of higher education in Western countries during the post-war decades is usually seen to have been brought about by policies attempting to provide greater numbers of qualified technical, scientific and managerial employees to meet the changing needs of occupational structures, as well as by political objectives to 'break down' class divisions and to put more open and egalitarian opportunity structures in their place (Halsey *et al.*, 1980).

Discussions of social mobility have also focused upon the industrialization process and patterns of economic development. It is sometimes argued that a logic of the industrialization process is an increase in the rate of mobility in society. In a sense, this is little more than a truism since, by definition, industrial growth will inevitably generate occupational changes and create jobs that will need to be filled. There will be structural shifts whereby industrial occupations supersede those located within agrarian sectors to become the core of the social structure. With the emergence of post-industrialism, brought about by changes in the technological and managerial processes associated with capital accumulation, there will again be structural shifts, with technical, scientific and professional jobs becoming more pronounced within the occupational structures. Again, this will affect social mobility rates (Bell, 1973). But what do these processes reveal about the nature of class relations? The answer is very little since such discussions, with their focus upon occupational changes, become removed from the analysis of social class. Notions of industrialization become detached from the discussion of class even though technological and occupational changes can only be fully understood by reference to the process of capital accumulation. It is the strategic decisions of senior managers, acting on behalf of shareholders' interests, that determine the direction of capital investment, the nature of technological change and implementation and, hence, the structuring of occupations. In other words, it is only by reference to the internal decision-making dynamics of organizations that occupational changes and, hence, patterns of social mobility can be fully understood.

Societies may be characterized by particular mobility rates but these are the aggregated expression of processes that occur within organizations. It is for this reason that explanations of rates of mobility steeped in analyses of educational systems are largely misguided. The acquisition of credentials, in itself, does not enhance an individual's mobility chances. This only occurs if these same credentials are in demand by employing organizations. In themselves, educational credentials are relatively worthless in terms of labour market value. It is the work processes of organizations that establish needs for qualifications and, generally, it is the function of educational systems to provide the means whereby these needs can be met. If the internal dynamics of profit-making corporations and other employing organizations are neglected, the *reality* of mobility experiences and processes is overlooked. But it is only in these terms that mobility patterns are meaningful. Only in studies of a relatively small number of 'elite' occupations, such as medicine, the military and the higher civil service, have the social contexts within which mobility rates occur been fully explored. Otherwise, the social constraints shaping individual life chances have been generally ignored. Some of these will be discussed later. In the meantime, it is worth stating some of the functions of mobility rates for sustaining the legitimacy of Western capitalist systems. It is, of course, the ideals of individual opportunity and the chances available for self-help that legitimates the 'open' and 'egalitarian' values of Western capitalism. It is in this light that entrepreneurship has ideological legitimating functions far beyond its significance as an economic process (Scase and Goffee, 1987).

The market, as it is associated with the capitalist accumulation process, offers not only abstract but also real opportunities for those who want 'to succeed'. Unlike state socialism, the capitalist dynamic and the availability of markets offer opportunities for those who wish to trade and thereby accumulate petty forms of capital. On the basis of their technical, craft or other specialist skills, individuals can trade with commodities or services in the market. The market rewards those who are able to identify market needs and it does so regardless of the social standing, qualifications and abilities of traders. Customer preferences are the ultimate deciders of trading success or failure and, accordingly, the market sustains within present-day capitalism the ideological promise and a complementary material reality of openness, equality and opportunity.

It is for this reason that entrepreneurship and business start-up now have widespread appeal. Although Western capitalism is characterized by an increasing concentration of ownership over the productive process, with quasi-monopoly national and multi-national corporations dictating the conditions of the market-place, the ideals of entrepreneurship continue to emphasize the 'openness' of the socio-economic order (Goss, 1991). They function to conceal the nature of quasi-monopoly control and the growing dominance that large-scale corporations exercise over economic activity. There are many examples of those who start their own businesses within specific market niches and later become wealthy and, indeed, the owners of large-scale corporations. Equally, there are several examples of well-known, large-scale enterprises originating from the efforts of opportunity-seeking entrepreneurs. Economic historians are frequently asked by such organizations to write their corporate biographies and, in these, the entrepreneurial skills of founders are often strongly emphasized.

The 'rags to riches' stories of Western capitalism preserve ideologies of openness and equal opportunity. Although such personal experiences are very rare, particularly under the conditions of contemporary capitalism, they are sufficiently frequent to be popularized and fashionable, and to sustain the dominant ideology (Hertz, 1986). At the very least, self-made entrepreneurs offer role models for others to emulate, albeit on a more limited scale. Within the context of personal networks and family relationships, the machinist who gives up a well-paid job to become a self-employed engineering sub-contractor and then later an employer with, perhaps, two or three staff is seen to be 'successful'. Through hard work and the exercise of the appropriate business skills, he or she is admired by others because of the ability to take advantage of the available opportunities. In Western capitalist society, then, the market is considered to be a place of opportunities; that is, for self-advancement and for personal material success. Hence, the petty bourgeoisie, consisting of the self-employed and small-scale traders, are functional for the capitalist dynamic of accumulation (Curran and Blackburn, 1991). Although for some they represent an earlier stage of capitalism, their persistence is to be explained by reference to not solely ideological factors but also material processes (Wright, 1985). For example, small-scale traders provide sub-contracting services, producing items and components for larger manufacturing concerns which would be less cost-effective if they were to produce them themselves. The growth of 'flexible' forms of organization and the tendency to 'put-out' the manufacture of components is indeed increasing the opportunities available for those who want to start their own businesses (Rainnie, 1991). Small traders are also able to meet the needs for specialist goods and services that larger corporations are unable to provide profitably. Thus the markets of Western capitalism are characterized by a greater variety of goods and services than would be available if only large-scale corporations provided them. Consumers enjoy a diversity of choice that is seldom available in state socialist countries, and as customers increasingly demand more specialist and sophisticated goods and services the opportunities for business start-up are increasing rather than declining. This trend is reflected in the growing numbers of individuals who are able to enjoy upward mobility and personal success through entrepreneurial trading in the market (Goss, 1991).

Many of these opportunities are taken by people who, for one reason or another, lack the credentials or personal qualities perceived by those in control of large-scale organizations to be necessary or desirable for appointment and promotion. Often, entrepreneurial ventures are set up by women, ethnic minorities and others who are marginalized and/or deprived in the labour market (Ward, 1991). Through developing these 'alternative' entrepreneurial personal strategies they are often able to enjoy better material rewards than if they were employed in large organizations. They are often able to make greater use of their talents and skills and to avoid the control structures inherent within large-scale corporations. The self-employed and small business proprietors, then, through the setting-up of trading ventures are able to obtain a greater degree of personal autonomy and independence. Other than the financial constraints associated with viability, they can determine the nature of their work tasks, regulate their pace of performance and, generally, determine the role of work within their life-styles. In short they can 'be their own bosses' and be removed from the control of others. But often entrepreneurship can offer more than this since it enables various forms of psychological degradation to be avoided. Within many profit-making corporations, prevailing cultures lead women and members of ethnic minorities to experience prejudice, humiliation and psychological injury (Allen and Truman, 1991). Thus, although the everyday reality of working within capitalism may have such personal consequences, the ideology and market-based structure of this same capitalism offers personal solutions to these system-generated processes. The mobile discotheques, hairdressing salons, car maintenance workshops, window cleaning services, fast food outlets, guest houses, private residential homes, nursing and secretarial agencies, and countless other small businesses set up by women, members of ethnic minorities and others, offer material and psychological rewards to those who are deprived and disadvantaged in their claims upon the rewards of large-scale corporations and the better paid jobs that are available in the labour market (Goffee and Scase, 1985).

Entrepreneurship, self-employment and engaging in independent trading legitimate capitalism and reaffirm its openness as a socio-economic system. The continuing persistence of an ever-changing petty bourgeoisie conceals the growing dominance that large-scale corporations exercise over commodity and labour markets. The ongoing reproduction of this stratum reaffirms the openness of class structure and the opportunities available through self-help and personal endeavour (Bechhofer and Elliott, 1976). Managers and others who exercise control over corporate resources have a readily available answer for those employees who express dissatisfaction with their employment conditions and level of wages; namely, it is their own choice. It is a 'free' market and there is always the possibility for them to start up their own businesses. According to this view, therefore, to be engaged in a working-class occupation is a function of a personal decision. Such views are, of course, at the very core of capitalist ideology and although the structural opportunities for such ventures remain limited, they are of sufficient frequency to sustain the legitimacy of such appeals. Certainly, there are large numbers of individuals who, employed in working-class occupations, know of family, friends and acquaintances who, in their terms, have become 'successful' business owners. As a result they perceive class boundaries to be open or even non-existent (Scase and Goffee, 1987). Such personal knowledge can encourage those who are engaged in working-class occupations to accept the predominant ideological view that social classes no longer exist – or, at least, that a person's class position is individually and voluntarily chosen rather than structurally determined. Such are the dilemmas that confront the leaders of working-class movements. Appeals to class consciousness that emphasize the nature of subordination and exploitation in large-scale organizations are often rebutted by people who have personal knowledge of those who, through their *own* rather than *collective* efforts, have circumvented these class relations.

The prevailing ideology of capitalism is more broadly based than this. Its origins may be steeped in rhetoric associated with classical entrepreneurial ventures in 'free' markets but, today, it encompasses a wider set of beliefs associated with personal achievement, credentialism and personal success through effective performance in large-scale organizations. Accordingly, the dominant ideology emphasizes a variety of *aspirational* values which, during the growth periods of the post-war decades, have shaped the attitudes and expectations of the working class. Two decades ago, Parkin (1971) suggested that modern capitalism was characterized by the existence of three major meaning systems: the *dominant*, the *accommodative* and the *radical*. The first expresses itself within the working class in either *deferential* or *aspirational* terms. Deference tends to be found among those who are working in small-scale enterprises and often living in traditional rural communities. Such workers 'defer' to the values and beliefs of their employers so that an 'organic unity' between employer and employees prevails. *Accommodative* meaning systems are located within traditional working-class occupational communities in which large numbers of workers share common, everyday experiences. In these, assumptions sustain notions of worker solidarity as located within existing capitalist employment relationships. Thus, only *radical* meaning systems, based upon working-class political parties and movements, express 'alternative' anti-capitalist values associated with socialist transformation.

These value systems have diminished in their significance as a result of various institutional and structural changes that have occurred within capitalism. Socio-economic changes, particularly those associated with the restructuring of capitalist production on a global scale, have led to the decline of traditional rural and urban industries and communities (Newby *et al.*, 1985). The contraction of large-scale manufacturing in Britain has led to a sharp reduction in the numbers of those living in traditional working-class communities as well as of those who are seen to make up the 'natural' constituency of radical political parties. Instead, patterns of geographical and occupational mobility associated with economic change have created community and work settings in which job performance and life-styles are more isolated and privatized. Accordingly, the dominant value system has become more pronounced within a restructured working class, so that *aspirational* assumptions are now more widely accepted within all social groupings. These emphasize the importance of self-help, individual achievement and personal success, with the consequence that traditional appeals to collectivism have been superseded by the ideals of individualism and personal aspiration. The 'openness' and opportunities available within capitalism are now more firmly entrenched within all sectors of society and, as a result, the legitimacy of capitalism as a socio-economic order is reaffirmed.

Such appeals, of course, help to deny the *reality* of class. Examples of personal success are well known within networks of families and acquaintances and so it is hardly surprising that sociologists have difficulty in explaining the relevance of class in everyday life. But this is largely because the criteria people use for defining 'success' are rather different from the measures used by sociologists, focusing as they do upon movements between sociologically constructed occupational categories. Notions of 'personal success' only have significance within the context of particular values and goals located within individuals' membership groups. Western capitalism has been remarkably effective in creating broad feelings of personal success within most sectors of society, with the result that the overwhelming majority of the population feel that they have a personal stake in its future growth. If a substantial proportion of those who are engaged in working-class occupations perceive that they benefit from the existing socio-economic order in terms of its opportunities and rewards – although perhaps not as much as they would prefer – they are unlikely to support political appeals for large-scale structural change (Marshall *et al.*, 1988). This is particularly the case if they interpret their own class positions either as 'freely chosen' or as the outcome of their *own* lack of competence in obtaining the necessary credentials for more highly rewarded positions.

In order to be 'successful' in society, it is not necessary to shift between occupational categories as required by sociological measures. This may be an important aspect of the mobility process but it is far from the whole story. Instead, people's evaluations of personal success can be determined by measures of personal consumption, life-styles and, importantly, home ownership (Saunders, 1989). During the post-war era real wages and, with them, the living standards of the broad mass of the population have increased. If measures of personal success are based upon these and if comparisons are made between family members and across generations, the overwhelming majority of people, including the majority of the working class, feel they have been 'successful'. It is only when cross-occupational comparisons are made that feelings of disadvantage and experiences of deprivation are felt. But how frequently are such comparisons likely to be made (Gilbert, 1986)? It is seldom that they will be made between occupational categories because these are rarely a part of personal reference groups. Individuals may compare their pay with immediate colleagues who, as individuals, are better or worse rewarded than themselves. Further, ideas about personal well-being or disadvantage may be derived from vague, media-based information about wage rates in different economic and industrial sectors. But generally these will be of limited salience except when trade union leaders attempt to mobilize the support of their members in pay negotiations.

It is for these reasons that the marked inequalities of Western capitalism are rarely challenged. First, there is little awareness of the inequalities. Second, there is little widespread concern among the *relatively* disadvantaged about them. Awareness of inequalities and deprivations tends to be expressed in terms of fatalism and general indifference (Scase, 1977). Certainly, the interrelationships between structured inequalities, on the one hand, and personal disadvantage, on the other, are rarely established, at least to the extent of generating widespread feelings of resentment and discontent (Lockwood, 1988). Hence, Western capitalism has been able to contain the infrequent challenges of radical political leaders and their more far-reaching reformist objectives. Working-class political parties and trade union movements have been forced to abandon their socialist goals because of the changing attitudes and values of their rank-and-file supporters. Personal acquisitiveness and broadly based feelings of personal success have led to declining support for radical political objectives, despite the persistence of class relations and the degree to which these generate glaring economic inequalities.

'Personal success', then, is subjectively assessed according to opportunities for self-advancement, which are generally seen to be abundantly available. Opportunities are not perceived as a stratified and structured feature of society. Accordingly, inequalities in opportunities are explained in terms of a variety of personal rather than societal factors, such as inertia, incompetence and lack of ability. Individuals rank themselves and others as personally 'successful' or not, and patterns of economic rewards are regarded as reflecting these individual differences. For those who do acknowledge the existence of class, it is seen to be largely a function of personal abilities and differences rather than of social relations within the productive process. As a result, social class and stratified economic inequalities are relatively impervious to radical challenges. The situation goes even further than this since, according to prevailing assumptions, economic inequalities are functionally necessary for sustaining the opportunity structures of Western society. Without them, individuals will not be motivated to succeed, and so they provide a vital connection between psychological motivation processes on the one hand and the functional needs of capitalism on the other. Individuals will not be prepared to undergo periods of training and sacrifice immediate economic rewards to obtain the necessary credentials for later self-advancement. Unless senior organizational positions are well-paid, there will be little or no incentive for individuals to cope with the demands required of them in strategic decision-making positions. According to such claims, it is relatively poor rewards that account for the low motivation and competence of technical specialists, managers and various experts in state socialist countries. The poor productivity and low professional commitment found in the former Soviet Union were seen as a direct consequence of its egalitarianism and, as a result, such problems can only be overcome through the introduction of market principles and greater wage differentials. In this view, economic growth, pro-ductivity and the development of professional and technical exper-tise are all dependent upon the existence of stratified inequalities. They are the determinants of individual motivation and instil per-sonal 'needs' that can only be fulfilled through striving for the most highly paid and, by definition, most responsible jobs.

The reward systems and opportunities structures of Western capitalist societies, then, are self-sustaining and mutually reinfor-cing. If there are allegations of injustice, these are more likely to be directed towards issues of opportunity than towards issues of economic rewards. Thus, notions of social justice become popularly equated with the availability of access to credentials instead of ideals of economic egalitarianism. It is frequently argued that because capitalism, in order to function effectively, needs various professional, technical and managerial skills, it is inevitably a more open social order than other systems. However, such claims dodge many issues, not least the persistence of traditional and inheritable forms of wealth and privilege. Although credentialism may be important, it is intrinsically interwoven with other social processes to produce structured inequalities in the opportunity chances of different groups. Indeed, these are stratified in ways that are highly congruent with those associated with the distribution of economic rewards. Those who enjoy economic advantages because of their positions with the class relations of organizations are in very favourable circumstances to pass these on to their offspring. Equally, there are similar patterns of inter-generational class inheritance among those who are economically disadvantaged and subject to the controls of others. At this point it is appropriate to discuss objective patterns of opportunity and to see how these are distributed, irrespective of the popular perceptions already discussed. As with economic inequalities, they are an expression of class relations. That this is not recognized within popular belief and is rarely part of subjective experiences does not detract from the matter. Indeed, it bears testimony to the extent to which dominant ideologies are capable of sustaining widely held assumptions about opportunities in capitalist society. Despite this, however, the evidence suggests that such assumptions conceal class rigidities in which there is a high degree of inter-generational inheritance of managerial and professional jobs on the one hand, and of manual occupations on the other. If there is any inter-generational openness it is among lower-grade technical, lesser professional and routine non-manual occupations. The relative closure of 'elite' managerial and professional positions is illustrated in Table 3.1.

Restricted patterns of recruitment into higher-grade managerial and professional occupations persist despite the fact that the numbers of these positions have expanded rapidly because of the changing human resource needs of modern organizations (Goldthorpe, 1980). With the growth of large-scale profit-making corporations and the associated expansion of state-owned health, welfare and educational institutions, there has been an increasing demand for employees who can exercise a variety of managerial, technical and specialist skills. Although some of these vacancies are filled by those of working-class origins, the greater majority are taken by the children of those whose parents are, or have been, employed in such positions. What accounts for this process?

As stated earlier, most sociological accounts tend to be steeped in discussions of broad social processes. As a result, the specific strategies whereby various elite groups are able to retain their privileged positions and, further, to pass these on to their offspring have been largely neglected. However, in considering these patterns, it is necessary to shift the analysis from societal processes to the more specific dynamics of particular organizational settings. In this way, it is possible to describe the procedures whereby

Table 3.1 Inter-generational mobility patterns in England and Wales, 1972

Father's class	Respondent's class (% by row)								
	I	*II*	*III*	*IV*	*V*	*VI*	*VII*	*Total*	*Number*
I	48.4	18.9	9.3	8.2	4.5	4.5	6.2	100.0	582
II	31.9	22.6	10.7	8.0	9.2	9.6	8.0	100.0	477
III	19.2	15.7	10.8	8.6	13.0	15.0	17.8	100.0	594
IV	12.8	11.1	7.8	24.9	8.7	14.7	19.9	99.9	1223
V	15.4	13.2	9.4	8.0	16.6	20.1	17.2	99.9	939
VI	8.4	8.9	8.4	7.1	12.2	29.6	25.4	100.0	2312
VII	6.9	7.8	7.9	6.8	12.5	23.5	34.8	100.2	2216
Per cent	14.3	11.4	8.6	9.9	11.6	20.8	23.3	99.9	8343

Based on Oxford Social Mobility Group. Sample: men aged 25–64 in 1972.

The classes are defined as follows:

I, Higher-grade professionals; administrators; managers in large establishments; large proprietors.

II, Lower-grade professionals; higher-grade technicians; lower-grade administrators; managers in small establishments; supervisors of non-manual employees.

III, Routine non-manual (clerical) employees; sales personnel; other rank-and-file service workers.

IV, Small proprietors; self-employed artisans; non-professional 'own account' workers.

V, Lower-grade technicians; supervisors over manual workers.

VI, Skilled manual wage-workers.

VII, Semi-skilled and unskilled manual wage-workers.

Source: Heath (1989, p. 54)

particular individuals become appointed to senior managerial, professional and higher technical positions. It is only within particular corporate and organizational contexts that the dynamics associated with patterns of recruitment and promotion can be fully understood. Indeed, such analyses require the understanding of intricate interpersonal processes as well as a grasp of the more important aspects of organizational cultures.

Rarely have interpersonal relations within organizations been considered by those interested in social mobility. A preoccupation with rates of mobility in society has led to the development of methodologies that are essentially quantitative rather than qualitative and that have an over-emphasis upon correlating the occupational positions of parents and children (Goldthorpe, 1980).

However, individuals are not simply allocated to positions in society according to a variety of mechanistic social forces. On the contrary, this allocation takes place within organizational settings according to the criteria and preferences of those in senior positions. People are recruited and promoted (or not) on the basis of criteria that lead to favourable predispositions towards some individuals at the expense of others (Scase and Goffee, 1989). Accordingly, credentials and competence are evaluated according to subjective interpretations (Kanter, 1977). This is particularly the case in the recruitment and promotion of those who are perceived to possess the appropriate 'qualities' for senior organizational positions. Corporate or institutional leaders have subjective notions of 'leadership' and 'management potential' as well as a range of other intangible, non-measurable criteria which they take into account. Senior managers inevitably determine 'the rules of the game' and control the channels of opportunity, against which any increase in the supply of qualified young people in the labour market brought about by the expansion of higher education provision may have little or no effect. Because of corporate leaders' predisposition to recruit particular 'types of persons' for management positions, a wide range of implicit but, none the less, class-related criteria become relevant in what is, essentially, a process of corporate sponsorship (Scase and Goffee, 1989). Since there is a tendency for 'like' to prefer 'like', it is not surprising that the outcome is the maintenance of a high degree of class inheritance in terms of the social characteristics of those who are appointed to management and other responsible positions. In this, however, there is no operative, explicit class conspiracy; rather, it is to do with personal preferences of individuals as these have been shaped by a variety of class experiences associated with schooling, family background and upbringing. Such factors affect individuals' attitudes, values, speech, dress and personal 'style'. Corporate sponsors and sponsored will share similar class experiences and possess forms of empathy and understanding that will predispose, often in very subtle and unconscious ways, the former to favour the latter in the organizational opportunity stakes. Those selected and later sponsored will be individuals perceived to possess the required 'qualities' for leadership. They will also be regarded as trustworthy, which, of all factors, is considered by senior management to be crucial for bonding personal relationships and the basis upon which 'effective' management can be established (Scase and Goffee, 1989). In this way, 'like' recruits 'like' according to a variety of subjective criteria that are perceived to be functional for the *rational* and effective operation of organizations. Thus the hidden subtleties of class determine the nature of interpersonal relations within corporate recruitment processes. As a result, class privileges are intergenerationally transmitted while, at the same time, they are hidden from public scrutiny and even legitimated because of prevailing taken-for-granted assumptions about rational managerial competence and effective leadership. Even though such criteria are class determined, they do not disclose themselves as such within organizational settings. Accordingly, class processes, real as they are within organizational selection and promotion systems, are not perceived to be either operative or relevant. Only individuals, and not class groupings, are seen to be pertinent. Nevertheless, the outcome is the under-representation in senior positions of people from working class origins, of women and of members of ethnic minority groups (Nicholson and West, 1988). Within most organizational settings it is possible to identify processes of 'sponsored' and 'contest' mobility, operating simultaneously because of the different competences required by the modern corporation. Men and women of working-class origin are likely to be destined to occupy middle and junior management positions, with their work assessed according to performance-related criteria. For those destined for the most senior corporate posts, however, personal sponsorship and patronage are additional factors that are nurtured within various 'informal' organizational networks and relationships. These more hidden but crucial dimensions of organizational life have been overlooked in most mobility studies.

Recruitment and promotion take place within organizations that have not only structures but also cultures (Morgan, 1986). The latter are more difficult to study because of their more intangible, less visible qualities. But this makes them no less significant in their effects upon mobility processes within corporate settings. A simple definition of organizational cultures could be that they describe 'the ways things get done'. Hence, just as organizations differ in the nature of their products, technologies, size, structures, etc., they also vary in their predominant values and assumptions (Schein,

1985). One of the responsibilities of senior managers in capitalist corporations is to obtain the commitment of their staff so that profit-making goals are achieved. Payment systems are crucial in this process but they are usually insufficient for sustaining employee morale. It is for this reason that it is necessary for senior managers to appeal to the psychological as well as to the material needs of their staff. The nurturing of 'strong' corporate cultures is an integral part of this and this is reflected in the fostering of particular core values and ideals (Ouchi, 1981). But what is most important about such organizational cultures is that, stemming as they do from senior management, they have inculcated within them beliefs and assumptions that serve two major purposes. First, they sustain the existing structure of class relations within work settings so that patterns of control, domination and subordination are maintained and remain unchallenged. In this, they are little more than dominant ideologies which reflect, albeit in subtle ways, such values as commitment, effective performance, competence and other ideals associated with managerial strategies for achieving their goals. Hence, staff are expected to reject the appeals of trade unionism, collective action and other ideas that may query the prerogatives and ambitions of senior managers. Second, organizational cultures sustain class-related values among senior managers so that they are part of the everyday reality of organizational life. In this, they have real consequences for the promotion prospects and career chances of all employees. Since the predominant cultures of Western capitalist corporations are derived from a variety of white, male, middle-class assumptions, it is little wonder that there are so few women and, indeed, men of working-class or ethnic minority origin in management positions (Kanter, 1977). As stated above, 'like prefers like' if only because of notions of personal trust-worthiness, and it is this, if nothing else, that integrates individuals into 'effective' management systems. Again, the outcome is a high rate of inter-generational class inheritance among those in such positions, particularly in capitalist corporations. It is only within state organizations that there seems to be greater representation of working-class men and women in management (Nicholson and West, 1988). The reasons have yet to be fully explored but this could be to do with their rather more meritocratic, credential-based cultures and, hence, the extent to which senior managers' discretion and their ability to exercise personal sponsorship is more tightly bounded through public accountability (Scase and Goffee, 1989).

Such factors account for the relatively restricted patterns of elite mobility that are to be found in capitalist society. Of course, there are other pertinent factors, such as the role of 'independent' professions and their methods of recruitment and training and, further, the financing and structuring of higher educational institutions. Even so, patterns of mobility in society are obviously linked to the structuring of class relations in modern organizations and these, in turn, are related not to explicit class strategies as such but to the attitudes and values of those who occupy various class positions. However, broader non-elite mobility processes have so far been overlooked and these will now be briefly discussed.

Essentially, the growth of large-scale corporations and related developments in modern technology have created needs for a broad range of lower managerial, technical-specialist and supervisory positions (Goldthorpe, 1980). As technological and administrative processes have become more complex, there are greater requirements for specialist skills and competences of one kind or another. Concurrently, there has been a declining need for workers to undertake different semi-skilled and unskilled manual tasks. The automation of work processes and the shifting of large-scale assembly line production to Third World countries has reduced the need for such routine manual labour. As a result, the changing skill requirements of large-scale corporations have created job vacancies which, in turn, have led to an increase in the rate of inter-generational occupational mobility in society. Hence, the children of industrial manual workers have been able to obtain various lower-grade professional, managerial and technical jobs. Their acquisition of qualifications within expanding higher educational systems, followed by vocational training, has enabled them to obtain more highly paid, higher status and relatively more secure jobs than those of their parents (Goldthorpe, 1980). Accordingly, they perceive themselves to be 'successful' and to have achieved occupational positions generally commensurate with their talents and abilities. For them, therefore, capitalist society is indeed 'open' because modern organizations offer opportunities, albeit of a limited kind, for personal success. It is because of this preponderance of 'mass' mobility that the 'closure' of elite positions is hidden and contemporary capitalist society possesses the paradox of being *both* 'open' and 'closed' in terms of its opportunity structures. Indeed, these contrasting patterns are clearly illustrated in Table 3.1.

It is hardly surprising that the level of class awareness is so low. Experiences of 'promotion', 'getting a better paid job', 'enjoying a higher standard of living', etc., do not generate feelings of class-based collectivism. Instead, they reinforce ideals of in-dividualism and of personal self-worth that are likely to negate the generation of class-related attitudes and behaviour. Nevertheless, the dynamics of class relations, as expressed in different organiz-ational settings, do have real outcomes for individuals' life chances. The fact that these are mediated through senior managerial strat-egies associated with the recruitment, training and promotion of employees explains why these class processes are normally hidden from public scrutiny. Hence, except among those with sociological understanding, the perception of Western capitalism will be in terms of its 'openness', 'equal opportunities' and general 'egali-tarianism', with a general feeling that 'class' is an insignificant feature of everyday life. However, this does not render notions of class obsolete for the purposes of explaining the *objective* structur-ing of opportunities in society. Indeed, it remains the case that there are people who continue to be concerned with the restructuring of society, and who recognize the importance of class not only as a determining variable in shaping life chances, but also as a mechan-ism for mobilizing collective action for social reform and social change. What, then, have been some of the responses to the patterning of class inequalities discussed in this and the previous chapters? This is the focus of the next chapter.

4

Class and Stratification: Some Collective Responses

Generally speaking, collective responses to class-determined in-equalities in patterns of opportunity and reward have been weak. Even during the 1960s and 1970s, when employer associations and political regimes were expressing anxieties over the growing 'threat' of labour movements, there was little evidence to suggest that working-class organizations were posing a fundamental challenge to the distribution of rewards in Western capitalist society. This is not to imply that collective organizations have done little to improve the working and living conditions of working-class employees and of various disadvantaged groups. Indeed, there do seem to be some cross-national differences in these that appear to be associated with the influence of labour movements (Esping-Andersen, 1990). But generally they have not constituted a fundamental challenge to prevailing class structures. In Europe, it is only in the former Soviet Union and the post-war Eastern European state socialist countries that political movements, claiming to represent working-class interests, brought about dramatic changes in class relations. These led to a drastic reduction in patterned inequalities compared with those found in Western capitalist countries (Lane, 1976), but with what ramifications for the structuring of social and economic institutions, the distribution of power and the constitution of civic society? In these countries, the dismantling of capitalism and the construction of state socialist institutions had socio-political outcomes that, in the 1980s and

1990s, have forced working class organizations in different capitalist countries to reappraise the nature of their 'socialist' objectives. It is useful to consider some of the factors that have inhibited the possibilities available to labour movements for restructuring the class relations of capitalist society.

As stated earlier, although the dynamics of capitalist society may create objective class relations, participation within these emphasizes *individualism* rather than *collectivism*. Despite the fact that employees may share common objective interests these are generally considered as less salient than those experiences that enhance personal feelings of individualism. Generally, people do not perceive themselves as class *agents* with their personal goals subordinated to class interests from which, in the longer term, they will benefit. On the contrary, personal anxieties, aspirations and emotions are the primary sources of individual motivation and, as a result, any form of commitment to a broadly based, class-related movement is likely to be perceived as secondary to personal self-interests. Thus, despite their objective location within class relations, individuals see themselves as distinctively different from each other rather than as sharing common interests as agents of class forces (Runciman, 1983). The institutional and ideological structures of capitalist society nurture such attitudes. By dint of birth and biography individuals regard themselves as unique in their personal and emotional make-ups. At the same time, the dominant values of capitalism emphasize how social structures are the consequence of individual actions. There is a widely held belief that individuals are bestowed with different talents and ambitions, with the effect that some will 'succeed' while others 'fail'. According to this view, the distribution of opportunities and rewards is a reflection of these individual contrasts. Similarly, socio-economic and political institutions are organized upon assumptions about the nature of human motivation. It is assumed that employees will not perform to their optimum unless they are individually rewarded through the operation of payment and promotion systems that must inevitably be inegalitarian (Davis and Moore, 1945). Similar notions shape prevailing ideas about inequalities in society in general, suggesting that these are not only inevitable and just, but also compatible with the needs of 'human nature'. This has had ramifications for the legitimacy of collective movements, the development of state institutions and the evolution of welfare systems since, according to dominant values, these are often considered to be contrary to the 'rights' and 'freedoms' of the individual.

The legitimacy of trade unionism in capitalist society has always been precarious. This is despite developments in the capitalist mode of production that have *objectively* created the pre-conditions for collective organization. The capitalist dynamic, during the course of the twentieth century, has brought about an increasing concentration of ownership and control within the accumulation process. This has led to the centralization of productive factors – labour power and capital – in large-scale industrial and administrative enterprises. The organization and management of these, permeated with assumptions about individual motivation and effort of the kind discussed above, has brought about standardization and routinization of work tasks, which has created favourable conditions for trade unionism and shopfloor organization (Braverman, 1974). The development of management practices described as 'Fordism' or 'scientific management', steeped in capitalist individualist values, created the circumstances within which trade unionism could flourish. 'De-skilled' workers increasingly lost their 'individuality' in the sense of their capacity to exercise judgement and responsibility in the execution of their work tasks. As a result, they became subordinated to common management control mechanisms, working conditions and payment systems. It is within such work settings that appeals to collectivism had and continue to have impact, with the effect that workers' attachment to trade unionism is relatively high; certainly by comparison to that found in smaller workplaces and where work tasks are less likely to be organized according to Fordist methods of managerial control. Indeed, it was within the larger 'Fordist' factories that trade unionism was often seen to constitute a fundamental threat to managerial prerogatives during the 1960s and 1970s (Piore and Sabel, 1984). It was as a result of this that senior managers within these large corporations developed a number of counter strategies, ranging from transferring productive capacity to Third World countries where labour was less unionized to 'robotizing' work tasks, abandoning the more extreme forms of Fordism and replacing it with more 'flexible' and 'participative' work practices (Wood, 1989).

Even in factories where Fordist principles are most pronounced and where trade unionism has obtained a high degree of worker allegiance to enable it to bargain effectively with management, it has failed to pose a fundamental threat to capitalist forms of ownership and control. Profit margins may sometimes have been squeezed and management may have been compelled to develop countervailing strategies of control but, on the whole, organized labour has been less effective than many radical writers would have hoped; certainly, in the post-war conditions of Western capitalist society. This is because 'individualism' as a reality of everyday life will always be more salient in personal consciousness than ideals of collectivism. This is compatible with the predominant beliefs of Western capitalism and constitutes the basis of liberal democracy as a pluralistic, participative political system (Mann, 1970). Political appeals are directed to individuals in terms of their *personal* circumstances and it is by reference to these that citizens vote and exercise their choices between political parties.

It is these factors, coupled with feelings of personal well-being and opportunity, that have sustained capitalism as a socio-economic and political order. Despite the many deprivations experienced in both the workplace and the wider society and notwithstanding the glaring socio-economic inequalities and the injustices of class encountered by many groups of wage earners, the development of capitalism within the twentieth century has, in absolute if not in relative terms, improved the opportunities and rewards enjoyed by the broad mass of populations. This, together with the ideological impact of capitalist ideals and assumptions, makes it rather surprising that organized labour, in the form of trade unionism and political parties, has been able to obtain the support that it has from the working class. It may be suggested that a major reason for this is the very *de*radicalization of working class movements that has occurred, since without this their precarious legitimacy would have been even more eroded than it has been during the post-war era of capitalist economic growth.

Much has been written about the deradicalization of working-class movements and the factors that underlie it. For some, the explanation is to do with the bureaucratization of political parties and trade unions, which has the effect that elected leaders and appointed officials cease to represent the interests of their rank-and-file members (Mann, 1973). This is largely because they become incorporated within negotiating processes and institutional structures, which affects their understanding of their members' interests. The outcome is the dilution of radical policies, with working-class leaders developing a vested interest in maintaining the status quo. Such a view is sometimes extended to emphasize how working-class leaders can exploit their positions for personal gain, an interpretation that has, of course, obtained greater credence since the developments in Eastern Europe of the late 1980s. In these, it seems that the abolition of capitalist orders led to the setting up of regimes in which party functionaries and so-called working-class leaders could appropriate resources for their own advantage and self-interest. That this did occur is likely to have longer-term effects for the political objectives of working-class movements in Western capitalist countries. Thus it is probably that, in order to obtain popular support, Western labour movements will need to abandon policies whose implementation would lead to centralized state ownership and bureaucratically organized forms of planning and control. The legacy of Eastern European socialism, with its tendency to totalitarianism and the curtailment of individual rights as expressed through state control over personal choice and freedom, has been to impose severe constraints upon the political objectives that Western working-class parties can now legitimately pursue. The full implications of the historical developments that have occurred in Eastern Europe over recent years, to say nothing of those within the Soviet Union itself, for working-class political movements in Western capitalist countries have yet to be assessed.

If there are those who argue that the deradicalization of working-class movements is a function of their bureaucratization and of their leaders pursuing interests removed from those of the rank-and-file, there are others who suggest that these movements have had to redefine their earlier radical goals because of the changing material circumstances and personal aspirations of their members (Marshall *et al.*, 1988). Since they are incorporated within the institutional and ideological framework of capitalist society, it is hardly surprising that this should have occurred. The economic growth generated by the class relations of capitalist corporations may exploit workers and enhance the wealth of shareholders. But this exploitative relationship continues to bring about improvements in the living standards of the broad mass of the working class. Despite fluctuations in rates of economic growth and periodic cycles of unemployment and, further, despite shifts towards greater inequalities in the material conditions of different occupational groups at different historical points of time – as in Britain during the 1980s – the absolute living standards of most workers have improved. At the same time, despite persisting divisions within patterns of opportunity and the ability of elite groups to transmit inter-generationally their privileged positions to offspring, the expansion of large-scale corporations, state institutions and more general forces of economic growth within capitalist countries has enabled increasing numbers of people to feel they have 'succeeded' and that they live within open, democratic societies – certainly, that is, by comparison with those encountered by their parents and previous generations of their families.

Because of the tendency for historical comparisons to be made in evaluating personal success and in shaping notions of well-being, structurally determined inequalities and relative differences between groups are seen as less salient. But even if such comparisons are made, they are likely to be by reference to more visible criteria than those associated with the underlying exploitative forces of class relations. Most people are likely to evaluate the rewards and opportunities of various groups in terms of such factors as ethnicity, gender, age, occupation, skill or qualifications, rather than according to social class. Even when such differences are recognized it should not be assumed that this will lead to feelings of envy and resentment. On the contrary, the values of individualism and self-help in capitalist society, together with their meritocratic claims, are likely to generate the reverse effects. As stated earlier, the disadvantages experienced by individuals are often attributed to their own failings and shortcomings rather than to the structural features of the socio-economic order (Runciman, 1966). Further, when workers acknowledge that they are objectively exploited within class relations, this need not generate – and, indeed, has not generated – intense feelings of resentment. This has only occurred in relatively isolated instances and, generally, class exploitation is regarded as a matter of fact, taken for granted as the reality of everyday working life (Nichols and Beynon, 1977). It is only when the overall costs of particular working conditions are perceived to outweigh the benefits that workers are likely to be predisposed to engage in collective action for the purposes of improving their lot.

If working-class movements have been able to sustain popular support, it is primarily because their leadership, to a varying degree, has been able to respond to the ideological and institutional changes that have occurred within capitalist society during the post-war era of economic growth. If, during the earlier decades of the twentieth century, the forces of structural change operated to the advantage of collective organization, socio-economic changes have acted to their disadvantage in recent years. This is shown by the trends in the level of trade union density in Britain (Gospel and Palmer, 1992):

1960	44.4
1965	43.7
1970	49.4
1975	53.2
1980	56.0
1982	53.8
1984	51.4
1986	48.8

Percentage changes:
1960–9	+1.5
1970–9	+7.6
1980–6	−7.2

The development of capitalism brought about the concentration of production within large-scale industrial corporations. This was necessary because of the economies of scale associated with Fordist methods of production. The de-skilling of work tasks encouraged the development of occupational solidarity and it was within such enterprises that labour unionism developed as a movement. Previously, it had consisted of little more than collectivities of skilled workers who tried to protect their economic self-interests through trade-based forms of collective action. But with the growth of large-scale corporations organized upon the principles of scientific management, there was a rapid growth of labour unionism among semi-skilled workers. These unions pursued the interests of employees in the workplace and of workers in society in general. In terms of the latter, alliances with radical political parties or the setting up of union-sponsored political parties were often pursued.

While the nature of class relations in the workplace established the preconditions for working-class solidarity, concomitant developments outside work reinforced this tendency. The process of industrialization and the expansion of capitalist economic production entailed rural–urban migration and the growth of large-scale urbanism. The creation of an urban proletariat brought about the workers' dispossession of their traditional means of subsistence, which were derived from petty property ownership and their traditional productive skills. Instead, they became dependent upon the sale of their labour power as the sole source of their livelihoods. With workers concentrated within rapidly growing urban areas, networks of social relationships emerged, which often incorporated work colleagues, neighbours and others who were subject to the similar class relations of domination and exploitation. Hence, the integration of common work and non-work experiences served to foster personal identities and social networks that emphasized the values of mutual help and working-class solidarity. The setting up of workingmen's clubs, workers' educational associations, trade unions and local branches of the Labour Party enhanced feelings of class affinity as well as the necessity of collective action if self-improvement was to be pursued. In this sense, therefore, working-class collective action, as expressed in trade unionism and support for the Labour Party, has been steeped in instrumental rather than ideological motives. With very few exceptions, there is little to suggest that rank-and-file members of working-class movements in Western capitalist countries have been committed to revolutionary political change. Commitment to labour unionism and to working-class political parties has been for the purposes of improving specific and particular work and employment conditions and of extending the role of the state in the provision of health, education, welfare, housing and social services. There have been virtually no rank-and-file demands for the transfer of private ownership, in the form of the nationalization of productive industries, to more publicly accountable organizations. Certainly, this does not appear to have been the case in the countries of Eastern Europe, Britain, Italy or France, where during the immediate post-war decades, nationalization was pursued as a political goal by working-class parties, reflecting the aspirations of intellectuals, party officials and leaders rather than of rank-and-file members.

If developments until the 1960s offered favourable opportunities for the growth of labour unionism and, associated with this, flourishing working-class political parties, these have diminished during the past decades. It was mentioned earlier that the increasing strength of organized labour compelled corporate managers to implement counter strategies during the 1960s and 1970s because of the increasing frequency of wage demands, unofficial disputes and union-sanctioned strikes. Profit margins declined and the economics of scale, one of the key features of scientific management, were not fully realized because of disputes over payment systems, productivity levels and worker output. In short, organized labour was perceived to be challenging the prerogatives of management and its methods of control. Rarely, however, did it aim to take over these functions; instead, its purposes were more instrumental and geared to the personal material needs of rank-and-file supporters. Nevertheless, management in large-scale corporations was forced to implement changes that, together with other ideological and institutional trends within the capitalist order, have undermined the pre-conditions for working-class solidarity. These have brought about the fragmentation of any previous semblances of class and occupational solidarity.

One of the more important of these has been the abandonment of the more rigid forms of Fordist principles of management control and their replacement by systems that extend responsibility, autonomy and working flexibility to employees. Through 'job enrichment' and 'quality of working life' schemes, managerial strategies for improving productivity and profit margins have been directed towards the implementation of high performance work systems, total quality management, just in time management, and so on (Buchanan and McCalman, 1989). With the adoption of these practices, the more extreme forms of the division of labour have been abandoned and individual piece rate systems abolished. In their place, a greater emphasis has been put upon team work, task flexibility and group-based payment systems. As part of such initiatives, there are attempts to obtain a greater degree of worker commitment through involvement in first-line management decision-making. As a prerequisite for the adoption of these managerial practices, there is often the setting up of 'single union' plants, sometimes on green field sites, so that traditional union loyalties are circumvented. This is reinforced by recruiting younger workers, usually school-leavers, who have few trade union loyalties. Such developments, although they may not prevent the formation of limited forms of worker solidarity in the shape of close-knit work teams, nevertheless inhibit the growth of more broadly based forms of worker solidarity (Wickens, 1987). Certainly, the roots of traditional trade unionism, in both their institutional and ideological forms, are eroded as corporate leaders, in their attempts to impose organizational cultures that are intended to emphasize the common interests of management and workers, revert to repackaged forms of industrial paternalism. Inspired by Japanese management techniques, which have been imitated by their American counterparts, senior managers are persuaded to develop a range of ideological and organizational techniques whereby workers are more inculcated with corporate values and ideals (Pascale and Athos, 1982). Thus, with the weakening of trade unionism, the exploitative nature of class relations within capitalist corporations is increasingly hidden by management rhetoric, although not entirely so, if only because the material circumstance of daily work serves as a reminder to both managers and workers that organizational consensus is extremely precarious and always subject to rupture.

These trends are being reinforced by a number of institutional and ideological changes that inhibit the appeals of class solidarity. The break-up of traditional working-class communities is being brought about by large-scale economic restructuring, the decline of manufacturing industries, population shifts between and within countries, town planning, urban renewal schemes and the spatial effects of 'improving' road transport systems in towns. The decline of the traditional manufacturing industry has been particularly significant in its consequences for labour movements since it was within this economic sector that the conditions of work and employment offered the most favourable circumstances for collective organization both within and beyond the workplace. But the decline of community and neighbourhood relationships, bringing in its wake the emergence of more privatized and individualized life-styles, has had important effects. The break-down of social networks has led to the destruction of personal support systems, which has reinforced the vulnerability of sections of the working class to poverty and economic marginality (Seabrook, 1984). This, in turn, has exaggerated their dependency upon state-financed health and welfare systems, their experience of which has added to their feelings of personal subordination. The provision of state services according to Fordist, bureaucratic principles has added to working-class patterns of economic and social dependency which, during the 1970s, nurtured a growing resentment towards state institutions and their provision of services of all kinds. At the same time, deprived groups have been compelled to develop strategies for personal survival, whether they are single parents, lone pensioners, homeless youths or the mobile unemployed in search of work (Harrison, 1985). Thus, structural changes have affected the nature of personal relationships and social networks and have led to a growing emphasis upon the values of self-reliance and the overriding importance of self-interest. This, of course, was quickly identified and nurtured by the Conservative Party in Britain, the Republican Party in the United States and other bourgeois political parties in Europe. In a sense, therefore, the emergence of the new right as an ideological force of the 1980s was an *effect* of structural changes in society rather than a *cause* of them. Once the new right became accepted as a major political ideology, its ideals became incorporated within political objectives that have had far-reaching effects for the material conditions of the working class. By exploiting its appeals to individualism and personal self-interest, it has been able to challenge the underlying assumptions of the welfare state and attack the ideological roots of political collectivism upon a broad front.

In the immediate post-war era, the growth of organized labour and its increasing economic and political influence brought about the development of socio-political orders that some commentators described as corporatism (McCrone *et al.*, 1989). In many ways, this embodies what can ultimately by achieved by labour movements within the parameters of the capitalist system. Corporatism consists of structures at the levels of the capitalist enterprise and the national economy, incorporating the interests of capital, labour and the state. In essence, it is a model of socio-economic and political organization that functions on the basis of collective representation and, in fact, corporatist structures are largely unnecessary when working-class movements are weak and underdeveloped. It is only when workers' interests become articulated within influential collective movements that it is necessary for capitalist interests to form employer organizations. This is particularly so when there are state institutions that also incorporate and protect the interests of workers. Although the state may be functional to the needs of capital, it also incorporates the interests of workers, if only for the long-term stability of the capitalist order. Whether the growth of the state during the post-war decades can be explained according to its functions for capital or in terms of its responses to working-class demands, it is evident that it does provide a range of collective services that benefit workers. Hence, it can be argued that the growth of the welfare state does reflect the increasing influence of labour movements, and when this power is curtailed, as in Britain in the 1980s, it becomes possible for the activities of the state to be cut back and for its role within the economy to be severely curtailed.

The decline of corporatism in the 1980s seems to be directly associated with the weakened influence of labour movements. Representatives of organized labour are now less involved in the governmental process and their contribution to national economic management has been acutely reduced. Accordingly, it is now argued that the state's only legitimate role is to provide a range of support services to the market economy, instead of the more 'directive' function it undertook during the earlier corporatist post-war era.

Such a change in the legitimate role of the state, as highlighted in the arguments of the new right, has had ramifications for the work and employment conditions of large sectors of the working-class (Hudson and Williams, 1989). Conservative governments, incorporating many of these values within their legislative programmes, have not only curtailed the influence of trade unionism and, hence, its capacity to negotiate effectively with management, but also repealed or weakened a number of legislative measures in such areas as health and safety, employment protection and equal opportunities. Further, the demise of corporatism and prevailing political notions that capital and labour should negotiate agendas of 'shared' objectives has removed from industrial debate the ideals of worker participation, co-determination and joint negotiation. If such values do persist, they are more likely to be found in large multinational corporations than in small or medium-sized enterprises. Even in the former, managerial objectives are overwhelmingly dominant, although often concealed within rhetoric that appeals to corporate loyalty, harmony and shared values.

The dismantling of corporatist decision-making mechanisms, at both the national and the company level, has curtailed the influence of organized labour and enabled capitalist self-interest to be more vigorously pursued in an unrestrained fashion. The post-Fordist flexible firm, in terms of its internal decision-making processes, is in many ways, an expression of this. Equally, the rapid growth of sub-contracting, franchising and the use of 'self-employed' workers on the basis of fixed, short-term contracts is a reflection of the ways in which management can pursue its goals unfettered by the demands of organized labour. An outcome of such developments has been the segmentation of labour markets into 'core' and 'periphery' or 'primary' and 'secondary' sectors. If employees in the former enjoy relatively secure jobs and acceptable working and employment conditions, the latter are more likely to be subject to deprivations associated with the temporary or uncertain nature of their employment. Without the protection of influential unionism and because the state has curtailed its interventionist economic role, such employees are left to pursue their own 'self-reliant', personal survival strategies. Trends in Britain during the 1980s suggest that the consequences are greater inequalities and the emergence of sub-strata within the working class of those who are economically, politically and socially disengaged from the institutional orders of society (Brown and Scase, 1991). In most of the countries in Europe, these sub-strata consist of semi-skilled and unskilled service sector employees, who tend to be women, ethnic minorities, school leavers and pre-retired older men.

It would seem that collective working-class challenges to class-related inequalities have been highly limited, particularly during the closing decades of the twentieth century. If in earlier periods the industrialization process created large-scale productive systems, which in turn offered favourable conditions for the growth of labour organizations, this no longer seems to be the case. If the major achievements of working-class political parties has been the creation of the welfare state and the establishment of post-war corporatism, developments in the 1980s have witnessed their demise. Hence, the roles of trade unionism and of labour and social democratic political parties have changed and they are now compelled to pursue very different objectives from those in earlier decades. Their commitment to equality, welfare and wealth distribution is unlikely to be embodied in the creation of centralized state institutions of the sort set up in post-war Europe. The large-scale nationalization of privately owned assets and the formation of state capitalist enterprises are no longer legitimate strategies for labour movements. Aims that emphasize the 'peaceful transition' from capitalism to state socialism are no longer on the agenda – particularly in view of the totalitarianism, political corruption and human degradation that characterized the former regimes of the Soviet Union and the Eastern European countries. Thus, the ideological and structural changes that have occurred within Western capitalist countries are having dramatic effects upon the strategies of labour movements. Developments in Sweden illustrate some of these, as well as demonstrating what labour movements can achieve for their supporters despite the persistence of structurally generated class relations.

Sweden, of course, is distinctive among capitalist countries in the extent to which there has been the development of a highly organized and influential working class movement (Korpi, 1983). At the beginning of the twentieth century, close collaboration between trade unions and the Social Democratic Party enabled them to develop coherent programmes of industrial and political reform. The rapid industrialization of the country in the 1920s and 1930s brought about the formation of an industrial infrastructure that was conducive to the growth of *labour* rather than *trade* unionism. Although the very early unions were organized on a craft or trade basis, the expansion of union membership during the inter-war years occurred in industries where Fordist managerial practices were being widely implemented. First generation industrial employees tended to be semi-skilled, working in large corporations. This, together with the absence of broader social divisions based upon such factors as language, religion and ethnicity, led to the emergence of a well-integrated labour movement which, in the

1930s, was able to bring about the election of one of the first social democratic regimes in the world.

Almost from its very beginning, the Social Democratic Party adopted an 'accommodative' or 'reformist' strategy towards the capitalist order. Its initial programme incorporated some revolutionary Marxist objectives, but these were soon to be superseded by policies that involved control over, rather than the abolition of, the capitalist economy. Since the 1930s, successive Social Democratic governments have implemented measures which have brought about the creation of a highly developed, state-financed welfare system and the setting up of a variety of corporatist institutions (Stephens, 1979). These, in their different ways, have ameliorated the more extreme aspects of capitalist class relations without abolishing the dynamic that sustains these same relations. Thus, the competitive process, inherent within the capitalist mode of production, has brought about a high level of monopolization with a very limited number of publicly quoted companies accounting for a high proportion of total output and employment. This process has been largely aided by Social Democratic governments, who have encouraged economic concentration through their policies of 'modernization' and 'structural rationalization', arguing that this is necessary if Swedish companies are to compete in world markets (Scase, 1977). Equally, Sweden is characterized by a class structure common to that found within other capitalist countries. Patterns of economic reward and opportunity are not fundamentally unlike those of other countries, which, in view of the discussion in the preceding chapters, is not entirely surprising (Davis and Scase, 1985). Although Social Democratic regimes have made use of state institutions and their control over the political decision-making process to bring about fundamental changes within the educational system as well as to introduce and maintain a progressive, redistributive form of taxation, these policies have not brought dramatic differences compared to other countries. What, then, have been the major achievements of the Swedish labour movement as expressed through the election of successive Social Democratic regimes? Essentially, the gains have been in the establishment of the welfare state and the regulation of the capitalist economy through the creation of corporatist structures. Both of these have served to benefit the material conditions of the working class to a far greater extent than in other capitalist countries. Although class relations have not been abolished – nor can they be without the abolition of the capitalist mode of production – the pursuit of different goals, utilizing state institutions as agencies for change, has improved the material and cultural conditions of the Swedish working-class.

This can be demonstrated by reference to a recent study, which has compared the development of state welfare systems in a number of different capitalist countries. In his analysis, Esping-Andersen (1990) constructs an index of 'de-commodification' according to which countries are ranked in terms of the ease with which individuals are able to 'opt out' of the market for the purposes of obtaining pensions, sickness and unemployment cash benefits. In other words, Esping-Andersen is attempting to measure the degree to which some of the more important aspects of welfare provision are freely and universally available and provided according to non-market earning criteria. Hence, he is attempting to capture 'the degree of market independence for an average worker' (p. 50). On the basis of this, he arrives at 'de-commodification' scores for eighteen countries, ten of which are:

Sweden	39.1
Norway	38.3
Denmark	38.1
Austria	31.1
Germany	27.7
France	27.5
Japan	27.1
Italy	24.1
United Kingdom	23.4
United States	13.8

Esping-Andersen argues that there are a number of factors which explain the differences, of which strength of labour movements is but one. However, he does suggest that this accounts for approximately 40 per cent of the cross-national variance found in the degree of de-commodification. Thus, it is evident that working-class movements, not only in Sweden but also in other countries where they have been able to capture the legislative process for substantial periods of time, such as in Denmark and Norway, have been able to

Table 4.1 Relative prevalence of long-term illness by social class in Britain and Sweden

Social class	Britain	Sweden
1 Managerial and professional	0.52	0.79
2 Lower managerial and supervisory	0.94	0.75
3 Routine non-manual	1.05	1.09
4 Skilled manual	1.14	1.18
5 Semi-skilled manual	1.23	1.21
6 Unskilled manual	1.38	1.20
All	1.00	1.00
Ratio of social class 6 to social class 1	2.65	1.52

Source: The Lancet, 1 July 1989

develop welfare provisions that are non-market based and enhance individual well-being and personal citizenship. This is a major achievement despite the fact that it may have little consequence for patterns of economic and social inequalities and for class relations in general. Indeed, it can be argued that, for most people, their personal health, economic security and pension provisions are considered to be more important than issues of class inequality. National elections are won or lost by political parties in terms of their strategies for such matters rather than broader class privileges and deprivations. It can be legitimately argued that the leaders of the Swedish labour movement have pursued the interests of their rank-and-file members in a highly effective manner. As far as health and illness are concerned, it does seem that there is a generally lower prevalence of long-term illness in Sweden, certainly by comparison with Britain, and that there are fewer class differences. This is, perhaps, one of the more important indicators of social reform since general levels of health in society reflect standards of diet, housing, medical services, education and the quality of life as a whole. Table 4.1 compares patterns between Britain and Sweden, demonstrating how there are a lower prevalence of long-term illness and reduced class differences in illness patterns in Sweden.

Sweden illustrates how working-class movements are able to

develop the state provision of health and welfare services to improve the material conditions of workers, but it also demonstrates how the setting up of corporatist structures is able to achieve a similar goal. By comparison with other capitalist countries, Sweden has a variety of national, regional and local institutional structures that, in their involvement with labour market policies and economic management, incorporate the interests of capital, labour and the state. They are concerned with various aspects of education and training, technological research and innovation, the quality of working life, economic and regional planning and, perhaps most importantly, the maintenance of an 'active' labour market. As a result, and this stems from a historical objective of the labour movement, the level of unemployment in Sweden is consistently very low. Whereas in many Western capitalist countries rates exceed 10 per cent, in Sweden the level of unemployment has rarely been above 2.5 per cent in the post-war era (Therborn, 1986). This has a number of effects, including enabling organized labour to maintain its bargaining capacity in its negotiations with capitalist corporations about wages, working conditions and the nature of corporate decision-making. At the same time, it leads to high employment participation rates for women, the disabled and many other groups who are often considered in other countries to constitute a 'reserve army' or 'marginal' labour. It also enables the Swedish labour movement to prevent developments that in other countries have led to the segmentation of labour markets into primary and secondary sectors and to the emergence of impoverished sub-strata within the working-class, of the kind found in Britain.

Sweden may be somewhat atypical among capitalist countries in the extent to which a well organized working-class movement has a high degree of political influence. Although it is a capitalist country with structurally determined class relations, the everyday experience of class is even less evident than in other capitalist countries. This enables Sweden to portray itself as the 'third way': as being neither a free market economy nor a state socialist country. It is for this reason that it is emulated as a model by the newly elected political regimes of Czechoslovakia, Hungary and Poland, despite attempts by the IMF and other funding organizations to impose more liberal capitalist regimes in these countries. A socio-political system has emerged in Sweden, based upon the existence of an influential working-class movement in a capitalist country, which ameliorates the extreme excesses of class and the market but which, at the same time, allows personal freedoms to flourish and citizens' rights to be protected. Within most capitalist countries, rightist political rhetoric emphasizes the essential contradictions between the 'state' and the 'individual', but the social democratic debate in Sweden stresses how the provision of state-financed collective services is a fundamental pre-condition for the enjoyment of personal freedoms and self-development. The Swedish labour movement has been able to maintain a level of legitimacy and political support that is the envy of comparable movements in other countries and which the September 1991 newly-elected non-socialist minority government will find difficult to challenge. It has pursued – and continues to pursue – policies that have enhanced the material and cultural conditions of its rank-and-file supporters. Although from a Marxist point of view these may be conceived as reformist rather than radical and, therefore, are often considered to be irrelevant for the pursuit of basic working-class interests, they have brought about social and economic reforms which have served these same interests but without abolishing the underlying forces of class relations. This may be the price that has to be paid if the alternative is the implementation of forms of state totalitarianism of the kind that existed in the former Soviet Union and in Eastern Europe. Indeed, this raises issues about the future role of labour movements in capitalist society. This will now be considered in the concluding chapter.

5
Conclusions

At the beginning of this book it was suggested that class is generally regarded by most people as being of little relevance for the understanding of the everyday lives. In describing themselves, people tend to refer to such characteristics as age, gender, ethnicity, place of residence, occupation, etc., rather than class membership. Most frequently, notions of class are used to describe inequalities in the past or related to aspects of 'status' or 'snobbery'. As stated earlier, it is only with the considerable assistance of interviewers that respondents participating in social surveys are likely to refer to themselves in class terms and to allocate themselves to one of a number of class categories presented to them. Other than for those engaged in radical political activity or academic social science debate, it is unlikely that notions of social class will have much meaning for the overwhelming majority of people. At best, class is a vague, residual feature of social life. This has ramifications for the general and perceived relevance of sociology as a discipline, if only because concepts of class are central to most sociological analyses in Britain. Since the overwhelming majority of studies, whether they are of industrial shopfloor behaviour, family relations, health, deviance or voting patterns, tend to be discussed in social class terms, barriers are immediately erected between the practitioners of the discipline and others. A consequence is that sociological discourse becomes introspective and, usually, locked into a variety of academic debates which are perceived by others as largely irrelevant to the description and understanding of everyday reality.

The essential argument of this book is that, notwithstanding the subjective reality of class, it remains a concept that is vital for understanding the structure of present-day capitalist society. To reiterate what has been discussed earlier, the capitalist mode of production cannot exist without class relations and vice versa. Without these relations no surplus value can be produced and accordingly, capitalism is unable to reproduce itself. Without capital and labour as productive assets, structured within relations of exploitation, capital is unable to accumulate. Hence, relations of exploitation are expressed as control relations and reflected as job tasks and responsibilities within the occupational structure. Class relations, and the changes that occur within control relations, are the underlying forces that determine the nature of job tasks, the delineation of work roles and the structuring of occupations. Work tasks do not consist entirely of technical or expert skills since they have built within them dimensions of domination and subordination derived from class relations. This is why it has been argued that sociological approaches which begin with analyses of occupations and then proceed to aggregate these into social classes are dealing with the effects rather than the causes. No understanding of occupations and jobs can be complete without recognition of their origins within class relations. Equally, the structuring of organizations, whether they are directly or indirectly associated with the production or realization of surplus values, can only be understood by reference to relations of control (Dahrendorf, 1959). Profit-making organizations and state-owned institutions are little more than aggregates of employment relations within which control is exercised by those in positions of authority over others who are compelled to execute a variety of productive and/or unproductive tasks.

It is for these reasons that the analysis of social class is important for understanding the dynamics of organizational change, related as these are to the development of the capitalist mode of production (Salaman, 1981). The inherently competitive processes of capitalism, bringing about the concentration of ownership in monopoly or quasi-monopoly forms, inevitably lead to the restructuring of employment relationships. Equally, technological innovation has repercussions for the nature of work and for the delineation of job tasks. But these processes cannot be fully understood unless it is appreciated that the underlying forces are to do with the production and realization of economic surpluses. They can only be considered within the framework of class relations and how the structuring of occupations and the delineation of work roles within organizational settings are determined by these. Thus, it is clear that the analysis of class is inherent to the study of capitalist society. Western industrial societies are capitalist and, hence, their economic development is determined by the interplay of class forces of one kind or another. The fact that the prime objective of capitalist corporations is to make profits means that they are characterized by relations of exploitation and control and, hence, consist of class relations. This is the reality of economic production, irrespective of the perceptions and assumptions of participating actors. It is for this reason that social class will continue to remain central to sociological analysis. To eliminate it would be to obstruct sociologists from the analysis of the core forces of socio-economic change as they exist in capitalist society.

This is not to imply that social class will be perceived by social actors as having much bearing on their everyday lives. In a sense, why should it? There would seem to be no reason for individuals to need a sophisticated understanding of the dynamics of class for the purpose of achieving their personal goals in terms of psychological and material well-being. Indeed, most employees do recognize they are exploited – although they may rarely use such an emotive term – but view this as a taken-for-granted fact of the employment relationship (Beynon, 1980). They accept that they are hired to perform tasks that will contribute to the profits of their employing corporations and that should their labour be seen by senior management as unprofitable or unproductive, they will be fired. Most workers see nothing immoral in this and many go so far as to query the value or efficiency of non-profit-making forms of economic organization. Hence, it is unlikely that an awareness of exploitation will lead to political activism and to a personal commitment to fundamental socio-economic change. As long as employees perceive that they receive 'fair rewards' for 'fair effort', that wage differentials are reasonably legitimate, and that they are able to earn enough money to meet their personal needs, they are unlikely to become engaged in collective action directed towards the destruction of capitalism. This does not mean that workers need be satisfied with the overall distribution of economic rewards and with the pattern of wage differentials (Marshall *et al.*, 1988).

Clearly, there is discontent, which becomes expressed in forms of industrial unrest, low motivation and wage demands. But such forms of protest are generally directed towards changes *within* rather than *of* the prevailing capitalist order. Equally, it is generally recognized that some groups in society are highly disadvantaged. But the explanations for this tend to be associated with personal failure and/or the actions of governments rather than with the inherent dynamics of the capitalist mode of production. Any targets of protest, then, tend to be governments rather than capitalist corporations.

If there is collective protest, it appears in terms of various occupational, industrial, community and, sometimes, corporate interests. Thus, social protest is inclined to emphasize divisions within the working class and can sometimes reinforce ties of solidarity that cut across class boundaries. This can occur when multinational corporations threaten to close particular operating units, with the effect that local management and workers will 'unite' in their protest. More generally, corporate restructuring, the introduction of new technology and structural rationalization will elicit forms of protest that are spasmodic and localized in particular work settings. To achieve heightened levels of class consciousness among employees has been the ambition of radical activists since the nineteenth century but, with occasional exceptions, this goal has not been achieved. This is not only because of the great diversity of personal experiences encountered by those occupying similar class positions, but also for two other reasons. First, the overwhelming majority of individuals do not perceive themselves as *agents* of class in the manner that radical activists would like. Thus, their own biographical experiences, structured as these are within the context of particular intimate relationships and personal networks, will be considered by them to be more important than broader socio-political processes, irrespective of whether or not these are class related. Second, in terms of an appraisal of personal costs and benefits, the great majority of citizens in capitalist society perceive themselves as beneficiaries. They may demand more in the form of enhanced living standards and improved working conditions but, on the whole, they see themselves as enjoying greater benefits than costs. Many see themselves as exploited and view the distribution of rewards as unfair, but they take these factors for granted on the grounds that it is a price that has to be paid for better living standards and for personal non-work freedoms.

This has been a major source of legitimacy for the capitalist order, but it has been greatly strengthened by developments in Europe in the late 1980s. In the closing decade of the twentieth century, there remains no viable alternative to capitalism. Even if it is accepted that the Soviet Union and the countries of Eastern Europe were not truly state socialist, but represented repressive forms of state capitalism or bureaucratic collectivism, socio-political developments in those countries have tarnished, if not destroyed, the notion of state socialism as a model for societal development. The repressive, totalitarian nature of these countries and their socio-economic structures produced forms of society in which the majority of citizens concluded that the costs greatly outweighed the benefits. Even if the official party orthodoxy was accepted – namely, that there were no exploitative class relations – the subjective reality for most people was one of subordination and the repression of personal freedoms, individual creativity, dignity and self-respect. In this sense, the abolition of social class provided little in the form of self-enrichment. People being viewed and treated by the party as agents of class forces bringing about the construction of socialism seems to have achieved little, except to have allowed self-recruiting elites to establish state institutions of repression and control. The legacy of the Eastern European 'experiment' of the mid-twentieth century has been to reinforce the legitimacy of capitalism as a mode of production and the acceptance of class and exploitative relationships *in* work as part of a taken-for-granted reality in societies that offer opportunities for 'individuality', 'self-expression' and 'personal freedom' *outside* work. Clearly, this has ramifications for the nature of sociological analysis as well as for the strategies of radical political movements. It is necessary to consider each of these in turn.

Sociology, as an empirical discipline, rapidly expanded in the 1960s when issues of inequality and justice were at the forefront of political debate. It was a decade when social democratic ideals were on the ascent and many countries in Western Europe had labour or leftist-orientated political regimes. It is not surprising that sociologists devoted much time and energy to the study of inequalities, both historically and cross-nationally. Class analysis became a predominant mode of sociological enquiry and, as a result, the study of capitalism became central in explanations of the structuring of inequalities within different countries. The outcomes of such approaches were many but, perhaps, the following are among the more important. First, sociology became seen, although perhaps incorrectly, as synonymous with radical political ideologies, orientated to fundamental changes in the capitalist order. Further, considerable amounts of data were collected documenting the widespread patterns of inequalities in Western capitalist countries. At the same time, there was a proliferation of a variety of Marxist perspectives, which became excessively theoretical and preoccupied with the delineation of class positions and boundaries (Parkin, 1979). But, and perhaps most importantly, what sustained the validity of these approaches and maintained the momentum of sociological class analysis was the *empirical reality* of non-capitalist countries in Eastern Europe. In other words, there was a real alternative to capitalism and so discussions of class, the determination of class boundaries, issues of class consciousness, etc., could be seen, implicitly if not always explicitly, to have a broader relevance than solely academic debate. Sociology was seen by some to be part of a wider enterprise to do with the transformation of capitalism into more humane, socially just forms of socio-economic organization. Even though the countries of Eastern Europe were not viewed as models – far from it, and many commentators emphasized their despotic features – they demonstrated that alternatives to capitalism could be established. In the 1960s, they constituted relatively novel forms of social structure, highlighting the possibilities of societal planning and social engineering, and the extent to which sociological findings could be applied in the design of social institutions. Even though they may have possessed many totalitarian features, for many observers these were seen to be a function of the need to industrialize rapidly, to defend themselves against counter-revolutionary forces and to become economically self-sufficient. Hence, such 'abnormalities' as totalitarianism and political repression would be resolved as the different countries of Eastern Europe developed into higher forms of state socialism.

In the 1990s, the 'failed' experiments of the Soviet Union and Eastern Europe poses a dilemma for sociological class analysis.

Thus, it is no longer credible for sociological investigations to be undertaken as part of a theoretical programme for formulating a strategy for societal change; namely, the transformation of capitalism into an alternative socio-economic order. This is particularly so, as it seems there is a widespread recognition *and* acceptance that class exploitation is an inherent and more or less permanent feature of society – as long as the benefits for the greater majority of individuals outweigh the costs which they or others may have to bear. Accordingly, the generally implicit belief of many sociologists that class relationships and, by implication, the capitalist order *ought* to be eradicated has now to be confronted in a far more explicit manner than in the past. At least this means that those who are committed to social change must proceed to formulate agendas for action which assume the continuing development of capitalism rather than its supersedence by an 'alternative' order. If it is to be accepted that class relations will remain a feature of society, the questions that have to be tackled focus upon issues of equity, distribution and compensation within societies where the essential dynamic of accumulation will continue to be exploitative. Thus, the focus of attention shifts away from hopes for 'abolition' to more detailed discussions about amelioration and social reform. It entails a return to the consideration of the ideals of Fabian socialism and, certainly, a collusion with the non-socialist strategies that are currently being formulated by some labour movements.

It has already been suggested that it would be counterproductive for working-class political movements to establish political programmes that appeal to class and feelings of exploitation. Even though these constitute inherent features of modern capitalism, they do not generate broadly based demands for their abolition. Hence, labour movements are now compelled, largely as a result of pressures from their rank-and-file supporters, to develop strategies that give pre-eminence to 'individualism' and to citizenship (Marshall *et al.*, 1988). State socialism, with its emphasis upon centralized planning and regulation, is no longer on the agenda and, in its place, there is a renewed appeal of social democracy, with its emphasis upon the market economy *and* the collective provision of various social and economic resources. This is the model which has been developed in Sweden, which is currently being applied in the Soviet Union and the countries of Eastern Europe despite economic pressures from many Western governments. While this model accepts the reality of class and exploitation within capitalism, it also recognizes that the state, as the expression of various competing societal interests, is able to ameliorate many inequalities and injustices of the sort found within liberal economies (Korpi, 1983). Hence, it explicitly recognizes that 'the market' allows for individual freedoms and self-expression but that, without state controls, this can lead to glaring inequalities and deprivations. At the same time, it admits that state socialism, in the absence of market relationships, allows for the gross abuse of personal rights and individual liberties. It is, then, not surprising that social democratic regimes have achieved little in ameliorating class-determined inequalities in patterns of economic rewards and opportunities. As long as market principles and capitalist accumulation are regarded as necessary for economic efficiency and for protecting individual rights and liberties, class inequalities will prevail. But this does not mean that such inequalities cannot be *compensated* by a variety of state provisions of one kind or another. Although both Swedish and South African workers may be exploited and, ostensibly, members of the working class, it would be naive to assume that their material circumstances are similar and that they share common interests. Plainly they do not, and even though class inequalities in Sweden in terms of economic rewards may be little different from those found within other Western capitalist countries, Swedish workers enjoy a greater variety of compensations than their counterparts in other countries; for instance, not only in terms of health, welfare and old age benefits, but also in terms of the quality of their working lives, their community environment and the general provision of cultural and recreational resources (Vogel, 1990).

Further, the development of social democracy has led to a shift in emphasis, from trying to change relationships of class to focusing upon the circumstances – the deprivations and disadvantages – endured by *individuals* occupying various class positions. Hence, reformist policies have been directed to the different social groupings that capitalist corporations, left to their own devices, marginalize and systematically allocate to the most disadvantaged jobs. Generally speaking, women, pre-retired manual workers, school-leavers, the disabled and members of ethnic minority groups tend to be given the jobs that are the least rewarding in terms of pay, opportunities and psychological satisfaction (Brown and Scase, 1991). In Sweden, these groupings have benefited from Social Democratic legislation, although they continue to occupy working-class positions. They remain exploited but are better off than their counterparts in many other countries because there is a state apparatus that effectively 'polices' the activities of corporations to ensure that legislation to do with equal opportunities, sex discrimination and minority rights is implemented and enforced. Although such social democratic reforms do not explicitly attack the exploitative relationships of social class, they ameliorate, if only partly, the more acute forms as encountered by the more vulnerable or marginalized groups in society (Vogel, 1990).

The effectiveness of such legislation is best illustrated by the strategies that the owners and controllers of Swedish capitalist corporations adopt in order to counter the effects of the reforms. Corporations have expanded their production or provision of services in countries other than Sweden. A number of Swedish companies have evolved into multinational corporations, not only because of the need to expand their markets but also in order to avoid the high production costs associated with manufacturing in Sweden. These costs are a consequence of the influence of the labour movement and of the extent to which Social Democratic governments have introduced legislation leading to additional expenses that have to be borne by employers. These range from holiday benefits and pension rights to the design and planning of workplaces. Swedish corporations have attempted to transfer many of their manufacturing activities to other countries in order to circumvent these. That this has not led to widespread protest by the labour movement is because there has not, as yet, been a big increase in the level of unemployment in Sweden and, with it, labour market conditions in which working-class gains would be seriously undermined. But this is a possibility and a constant reminder to workers of their vulnerability in capitalist society because of their dependency upon the sale of their labour power.

In view of developments in the Soviet Union and Eastern Europe during the late 1980s and 1990s it would seem that capitalism and its inherent class relationships are now better legitimated than at any previous time. In none of the mature capitalist countries are there viable, broadly supported revolutionary movements and, as a result, *reformist* or *compensatory* strategies of the kind pursued in Sweden are likely to be the predominant strategies of labour movements. Class and capitalism are likely to remain long-term, almost permanent, features of industrial societies and, hence, debate should no longer be about the abolition of social class but about other important factors. There are three of these that may be singled out. First is the distribution of rewards as these are allocated to different occupational positions. What is an 'equitable' reward system and according to what kinds of criteria should economic inequalities be determined? In most Western capitalist countries, the present-day distribution of economic rewards appears to be irrational and, according to most moral values, offensive. Accepting the continuing existence of capital and class, how can class inequalities be more publicly accountable and equitably determined? Second is the allocation of individuals to occupational positions. How, and according to what criteria, are occupational positions to be allocated? Should not the selection and promotion policies of senior managers in large-scale organizations be subject to closer scrutiny, if only because the occupational aspirations of deprived groups in society are becoming more pronounced? Third, assuming the continuing persistence of class and capitalism, how should those who are allocated to the worst paid and most demeaning occupational positions be compensated by collective provisions of one kind or another? This raises questions about the role of the state, in terms of both its intervention in the market economy and the method of provision of its services for those who are in need.

In sum, the tackling of such issues implies the further development of the 'mixed economy', the 'third way' 'welfare capitalism' in societies where the influence of labour movements is recognized and their legitimacy is sustained. Further, it assumes a high degree of state intervention in both the productive and the distributive processes. The adoption of corporatist forms of socio-political organization, then, would seem to offer a viable strategy for labour movements that want both to ameliorate the more extreme excesses of exploitation found in liberal democratic capitalist societies and, at the same time, to avoid the oppressive totalitarianism of the former state socialist countries. None of this, of course, is new; it is to be found in the ideals of traditional Fabian socialism, the programmes of the Scandinavian Social Democratic parties and some of the political assumptions of the 1960s. What is required, however, is for Marxist sociologists to address these issues more seriously rather than, as they have over the past three decades, to dismissing them as being generally peripheral to the fundamental analysis of class relations.

Social class is part of the inherent reality of capitalist society and, for sociologists, it is an essential component of their analytical framework for understanding social structures and processes. Thus, the use of Marxist categories has been, and will continue to be, invaluable. However, to share with Marx his ideas for abolishing class must, towards the end of the twentieth century, be seen to be Utopian. In accepting both the reality and the relative permanence of class, it is now appropriate for sociologists to shift their emphasis from abstract theoretical paradigms that would seem to have little practical or political meaning. The overwhelming majority of people in capitalist society accept the personal costs of class exploitation because it offers them compensatory benefits. Eastern European state socialism failed to do this. Western capitalism is characterized by relations of exploitation but it is also distinguished by the opportunities it offers for rights of citizenship. Therein lies its paradox, the collapse of Soviet and Eastern European state socialism, and the longer-term legitimacy of social class and capitalism. It is the rise and fall of state socialism which the twentieth century has witnessed rather than the demise of capitalism. The question is no longer whether or not capitalism but of what variety or type.

Bibliography

Abercrombie, N. and Urry, J. (1983). *Capital, Labour and the Middle Classes*. London: Allen and Unwin.

Allen, S. and Truman, C. (1991). 'Prospects for women's business and self-employment in the year 2000', in J. Curran and R. Blackman (eds) *Paths of Enterprise: the Future of the Small Business*. London: Routledge.

Anthony, F. (1986). *The Foundation of Management*. London: Tavistock.

Atkinson, J. and Meager, N. (1985). *Changing Working Patterns*. London: NEDO.

Baran, B. (1988). 'Office automation and women's work: the technological transformation of the insurance industry', in R. Pahl (ed.) *On Work*. Oxford: Basil Blackwell.

Bechhofer, F. and Elliot, B. (1976). 'Persistence and change: the petite bourgeoisie in industrial society', *European Journal of Sociology*, **17**.

Bell, D. (1973). *The Coming of Post-Industrial Society*. New York: Basic Books.

Bendix, R. (1956). *Work and Authority in Industry*. New York: Basic Books.

Beynon, H. (1980). *Working For Ford*. Wakefield: EP Publishing.

Braverman, H. (1974). *Labour and Monopoly Capital*. New York: Monthly Review Press.

Brown, P. and Scase, R. (eds) (1991). *Poor Work: Disadvantage and the Division of Labour*. Milton Keynes: Open University Press.

Buchanan, D. and McCalman, J. (1989). *High Performance Work Systems*. London: Routledge.

Carchedi, G. (1975). 'On the economic identification of the new middle class', *Economy and Society*, **4**.

Central Statistical Office (1988). *Social Trends*. London: HMSO.

Child, J. (1988). 'Managerial strategies, new technology and the labour process', in R. Pahl (ed.) *On Work*. Oxford: Basil Blackwell.

Cockburn, C. (1986). 'Women and technology: opportunity is not enough', in K. Purcell, S. Wood, A. Waton and S. Allen (eds) *The Changing Experience of Employment*. London: Macmillan.

Confederation of British Industry (1990). *A Nation of Shareholders: Report of the CBI Wider Share Ownership Task Force*. London.

Crompton, R. and Jones, G. (1984). *White Collar Proletariat*. London: Macmillan.

Crompton, R. and Reid, S. (1982). 'The deskilling of clerical work', in S. Wood (ed.) *The Degradation of Work?* London: Hutchinson.

Curran, J. and Blackburn, R. (1991). 'Changes in the context of enterprise: some socio-economic and environmental factors facing small firms in the 1990s', in J. Curran and R. Blackburn (eds) *Patterns of Enterprise: the Future of the Small Business*. London: Routledge.

Dahrendorf, R. (1959). *Class and Class Conflict in Industrial Society*. London: Routledge and Kegan Paul.

Davis, H. and Scase, R. (1985). *Western Capitalism and State Socialism: an Introduction*. Oxford: Basil Blackwell.

Davis, K. and Moore, W. (1945). 'Some principles of stratification', *American Sociological Review*, **10**.

de Vroey, M. (1980). 'A Marxist view of ownership and control', in T. Nichols (ed.) *Capital and Labour*. London: Fontana.

Edwards, R. (1979). *The Contested Terrain*. London: Heinemann.

Erikson, R. (1984). 'Social class of men, women and families', *Sociology*, **18**.

Esping-Andersen, G. (1990). *The Three Worlds of Welfare Capitalism*. Cambridge: Polity Press.

Gallie, D. (ed.) (1988). *Employment in Britain*. Oxford: Basil Blackwell.

Gilbert, M. (1986). *Inflation and Social Conflict*. Brighton: Wheatsheaf Books.

Goffee, R. and Scase, R. (1985). *Women in Charge: the Work and Life Styles of Female Entrepreneurs*. London: George Allen and Unwin.

Goldthorpe, J. (1980). *Social Mobility and Class Structure in Modern Britain*. Oxford: Clarendon Press.

Goldthorpe, J. (1983). 'Women and class analysis: in defence of the conventional view', *Sociology*, **17**.

Gospel, H. and Palmer, G. (1992). *British Industrial Relations*. London: Harper Collins.

Goss, D. (1991). *Small Business and Society*. London: Routledge.

Halsey, A. (1986). *Change in British Society*, 3rd edn. Oxford: Oxford University Press.

Halsey, A., Heath, A. and Ridge, J. (1980). *Origins and Destinations: Family, Class and Education in Modern Britain*. Oxford: Clarendon Press.

Hamilton, M. and Hirszowicz, M. (1987). *Class and Inequality in Pre-industrial Capitalist and Communist Societies*. London: Harvester Wheatsheaf.

Hannah, L. and Kay, J. (1977). *Concentration in Modern Industry*. London: Macmillan.

Harrison, P. (1985). *Inside the Inner City*. Harmondsworth: Penguin.

Heath, A. (1981). *Social Mobility*. London: Fontana.

Heath, A. and McDonald, S. (1987). 'Social change and the future of the left'. *Political Quarterly*, **58**.

Hertz, L. (1986). *The Business Amazons*. London: Andre Deutsch.

Hudson, R. and Williams, A. (1989). *Divided Britain*. London: Belhaven Press.

Ingham, G. (1984). *Capitalism Divided? The City and Industry in British Social Development*. London: Macmillan.

Jones, B. (1989). 'When certainty fails: inside the factory of the future', in S. Wood (ed.) *The Transformation of Work*. London: Unwin Hyman.

Kanter, R. (1977). *Men and Women of the Corporation*. New York: Basic Books.

Kerr, K., Harrison, F. and Myers, C. (1960). *Industrialism and Industrial Man*. Cambridge, MA: Harvard University Press.

Korpi, W. (1983). *The Democratic Class Struggle*. London: Routledge and Kegan Paul.

Labour Research (1987). 'Big fish grab sell-off shares', *Labour Research*, September.

Lane, D. (1976). *The Socialist Industrial State: towards a Political Sociology of State Socialism*. London: Allen and Unwin.

Lockwood, D. (1988). 'The weakest link in the chain? Some comments on the Marxist theory of action', in D. Rose (ed.) *Social Stratification and Economic Change*. London: Hutchinson.

McCrone, D., Elliot, B. and Bechhofer, F. (1989). 'Corporatism and the new right', in R. Scase (ed.) *Industrial Societies: Crisis and Division in Western Capitalism and State Socialism*. London: Unwin Hyman.

Mann, M. (1970). 'The social cohesion of liberal democracy', *American Sociological Review*, **35**.

Mann, M. (1973). *Consciousness and Action among the Western Working Class*. London: Macmillan.

Marglin, S. (1980). 'What do bosses do? The origins and functions of hierarchy in capitalist production', in T. Nichols (ed.) *Capital and Labour*. London: Fontana.

Marshall, G., Newby, H., Rose, R. and Vogler, C. (1988). *Social Class in Modern Britain*. London: Hutchinson.

Marx, K. (1974). *Capital*, 3 vols. London: Lawrence and Wishart.

Marx, K. (1975). 'Preface to a contribution to the critique of political economy', in *Karl Marx: Early Writings*. Harmondsworth: Penguin.

Marx, K. and Engels, F. (1964). *Pre-Capitalist Economic Formations*. London: Lawrence and Wishart.

Marx, K. and Engels, F. (1969). *The Communist Manifesto*. Harmondsworth: Penguin.

Mills, C. W. (1951). *White Collar*. New York: Oxford University Press.

Morgan, G. (1986). *Images of Organization*. London: Sage Publications.

Murray, F. (1988). 'The decentralization of production – the decline of the mass-collective worker?', in R. Pahl (ed.) *On Work*. Oxford: Basil Blackwell.

Newby, H. *et al.*, (1985). 'From class structure to class action: British working-class politics in the 1980s', in B. Roberts *et al.*, (eds) *New Approaches to Economic Life*. Manchester: Manchester University Press.

Nichols, T. and Beynon, H. (1977). *Living with Capitalism*. London: Routledge and Kegan Paul.

Nicholson, N. and West, M. (1988). *Managerial Job Change: Men and Women in Transition*. Cambridge: Cambridge University Press.

Offe, C. (1976). *Industry and Inequality*. London: Edward Arnold.

Ouchi, W. (1981). *Theory Z: How American Business Can Meet the Japanese Challenge*. Reading, MA: Addison-Wesley.

Pahl, R. (1984). *Divisions of Labour*. Oxford: Basil Blackwell.

Parkin, F. (1971). *Class Inequality and Political Order*. London: MacGibbon and Kee.

Parkin, F. (1979). *Marxism and Class Theory*. London: Tavistock.

Pascale R. and Athos, A. (1982). *The Art of Japanese Management*. Harmondsworth: Penguin.

Piore, M. and Sabel, C. (1984). *The Second Industrial Divide: Possibilities for Prosperity*. New York: Basic Books.

Pond, C. (1989). 'The changing distribution of income, wealth and poverty', In C. Hamnett, L. McDowell and P. Sarre (eds) *The Changing Social Structure*. London: Sage Publications.

Poulantzas, N. (1975). *Classes in Contemporary Capitalism*. London: New Left Books.

Rainnie, A. (1991). 'Small firms: between the enterprise culture and "New Times"', in R. Burrows (ed.) *Deciphering the Enterprise Culture*. London: Routledge.

Runciman, W. (1966). *Relative Deprivation and Social Justice*. London: Routledge and Kegan Paul.

Runciman, W. (1983). 'Capitalism without classes', *British Journal of Sociology*, **34**.

Sabel, C. (1982). *Work and Politics: the Division of Labour in Industry.* Cambridge: Cambridge University Press.

Salaman, G. (1981). *Class and the Corporation.* London: Fontana.

Sarre, P. (1989). 'Recomposition of the class structure', in C. Hamnett, C. McDowell and P. Sarre (eds) *Re-Structuring Britain: the Changing Social Structure.* London: Sage Publications.

Saunders, P. (1989). *A Nation of Homeowners.* London: Unwin Hyman.

Scase, R. (1977). *Social Democracy in Capitalist Society.* London: Croom Helm.

Scase, R. and Goffee, R. (1987). *The Real World of the Small Business Owner.* London: Croom Helm.

Scase, R. and Goffee, R. (1989). *Reluctant Managers: Their Work and Life Styles.* London: Unwin Hyman.

Schein, E. (1985). *Organizational Culture and Leadership.* San Fransisco: Jossey-Bass.

Scott, J. (1985). *Corporations, Classes and Capitalism.* London: Hutchinson.

Seabrook, J. (1984). *The Idea of Neighbourhood.* London: Pluto Press.

Stanworth, M. (1984). 'Women and class analysis: a reply to Goldthorpe', *Sociology*, **18**.

Stephens, J. (1979). *The Transition from Capitalism to Socialism.* London: Macmillan.

Therborn, G. (1986). *Why Some People Are More Unemployed than Others.* London: Verso.

Vogel, J. (1990). *Lev i Norden* (Living Conditions in Scandinavia). Stockholm: Nordic Statistical Secretariat.

Ward, R. (1991). 'Economic development and ethnic business', in J. Curran and R. Blackburn (eds) *Paths of Enterprise: the Future of the Small Business.* London: Routledge.

Weber, M. (1968). *Economy and Society.* New York: Bedminster Press.

Wickens, P. (1987). *The Road to Nissan.* London: Macmillan.

Wood, S. (1989). 'The transformation of work', in S. Wood (ed.) *The Transformation of Work.* London: Unwin Hyman.

Wright, E. O. (1976). 'Contradictory class locations', *New Left Review*, **98**.

Wright, E. O. (1985). *Classes.* London: Verso.

Wright, E. O. *et al.*, (1982). 'The American class structure', *American Sociological Review*, **47**.

Index